LAWN
PERFECTION!

**A GOLF COURSE
SUPERINTENDENTS GUIDE TO HOME**

LAWN CARE &
MAINTENANCE

BILL BROWN

CONTENTS

INTRO

It's early morning, and I'm out on the golf course, getting ready for another busy day. I start by walking the fairways, making sure everything is in order. But as I walk, I notice something strange. The grass isn't looking right and it appears like certain spots are covered by some type of fungus.

I start to feel a sense of dread as I realize how quickly this could get out of control. Yesterday everything was in order and today, I have a major problem on my hands before I even have a chance to sip my morning coffee. This is the life of a golf course superintendent.

If I don't immediately address the problem, it could mean having to close part of the course down for treatment, which would be a big blow to the club and a disappointment to all the members and guests who love to play here. It is on me to solve this problem and make it seem like it never happened.

Upon further analysis, with a spot spraying fungicide the problem should be under control. We'll know for sure whether the treatment worked over the next couple of days. Every divot left unrepaired, every blade of yellow grass, every fairway that isn't absolutely perfect, and every green that isn't as smooth as silk absolutely pesters the perfectionist in me. I'll be honest, I'm glad this phase of my life has passed.

While I loved my job as golf course superintendent, it was quite stressful. However, watching golfers smile as they step up to the first tee-off, knowing this round will be a memorable experience, was worth every ounce of effort.

Every challenge I had to deal with on the golf course was just another valuable lesson, another notch in the belt of knowledge. I am honored to be able to share this knowledge with you in *Lawn Perfection! A Golf Course Superintendent's Guide To Home Lawn Care And Maintenance* so your grass can be the shining beacon in your neighborhood. An absolutely perfect lawn, something that many strive for, but only a few achieve, is within reach.

Imagine yourself waking up every day, stepping out onto your green, lush lawn, and taking in a big breath of fresh air. As you wave to your neighbor and then look back at your lawn you already know it is going to be another good day. There is no sensation more fulfilling than knowing that you put in the effort to bring your lawn up to the level where it is fit for a king.

On that note, the origins of the modern-day lawn stem back to the 17th century when royalty and wealthy landowners were the first to plant grass. Before the advent of the lawnmower, only the very richest could afford to pay laborers to tend to their grass so a perfectly manicured lawn was a status symbol. Little has changed today, as the perfectly maintained lawn is still a symbol of prestige. Fortunately, we do have the lawnmower and plenty of other machines so we can take it upon ourselves to care for our own lawn.

Enough chatter and fantasizing, it is time to get to work, as maintaining the perfect lawn require continuous effort. However, for most of us who love the smell of freshly cut grass, it doesn't feel like work. Yes, it is physically demanding, but also extremely rewarding. You have nearly complete control of your lawn, and the amount of effort you are willing to put into it will be returned to you year after year. The peace of mind you will feel when you step outside of your house and touch your flawless grass is indescribable.

You Will Soon Know Exactly How That Feels.

I am going to show you the step-by-step process of lawn care and maintenance. I know exactly what works and what doesn't after so many years in this field.

I am going to explain to you why most homeowners don't have the perfect lawn even if they are willing to put in the effort.

You are going to learn about the common beginner mistakes that you are making and simple solutions to correct those errors so your lawn looks perfect.

Just follow the information in this book and you will have a beautiful, green lawn with no dry spots, yellow spots, weeds, pests, or diseases.

My name is Bill Brown and I was a golf course superintendent for 10 years. I have moved on from that profession but my passion for lawn care is still part of who I am. I wrote this book to help you achieve the perfect lawn without wasting time and committing the same mistakes I did at the beginning. I am going to show you the right way to improve and maintain your lawn correctly the first time so you will see immediate, lasting results.

While achieving lawn perfection may seem like a daunting task, it's actually quite simple if you follow some basic guidelines. In this book, I'll share my insider tips and tricks for achieving a perfectly manicured lawn.

For me, lawn maintenance is a pleasure because it has been my life-long passion. I am honored to share this information with you so you can take your lawn into your own hands and make it look better than most professionally manicured lawns. Simply follow the information I present in this book and you will have the lawn of your dreams.

Lawn Perfection! A Golf Course Superintendent's Guide To Home Lawn Care And Maintenance is a comprehensive guide to lawn care that covers everything from choosing a suitable grass for your lawn, to planting, renovating, mowing, watering, and fertilizing your lawn. This book also includes tips on dealing with common lawn problems such as weeds, pests, and diseases. Whether you're a beginner or an experienced landscaper, I guarantee you that this book will change your perspective on lawn care.

Ready? Let's go! Your perfect lawn awaits.

CHAPTER 1 - CHOOSING THE RIGHT GRASS SEED FOR YOUR YARD

There are tens of thousands of different grass species, from sugarcane to bamboo, but only a few of those are appropriate for your lawn. These select species are known as turfgrass. Turfgrass is unique in that it grows in a compact format and actually enjoys being mowed, whereas other grasses prefer to grow as tall as possible. Selecting the best turfgrass for your lawn is the key to a lush green color, limited wear resistance, and texture.

Here we are at the beginning, and I'll assume you are also starting at the beginning with a dirt-filled lot. You are probably thinking, what type of grass should I plant? While it seems easy, choosing the right grass genetics for your lawn can get complicated if you are determined to have the best lawn imaginable.

Choosing The Best Type Of Grass To Plant

There are a number of different types of grass seeds that you can choose for your lawn, and the type of grass that you should choose will ultimately depend on your personal preferences. If you want a low-maintenance lawn, then you might want to consider selecting a type of grass that is known for being easy to care for. Conversely, if you are willing to put in the work to maintain a lush, green lawn, then you might want to consider a more high-maintenance type of grass.

Ask yourself, what are your goals with your lawn? Do you want a lawn that is absolutely perfect? Do you want a lawn where you can throw the baseball around with your kids? Do you want a lawn where you can set up a bonfire in your backyard and have your friends over? Your lifestyle should determine the type of lawn grass species you ultimately decide to plant.

Furthermore, your climate has a lot to do with the type of grass you can grow and which is best for your situation. Let's take a look at the best types of grass for warm climates, cold climates, and the transition zone that spans east to west across the center of the United States.

While it may seem like all grass seeds are simply the same, the scientific advancements in creating new, desirable cultivars have given rise to grass genetics that is infinitely better than typical store-bought grass seeds. The genetics behind the grass seed you plant will ultimately determine your lawn's potential. There is no replacement for ideal genetics so research the most desirable grass seeds that can be planted in your region and spend the extra money to get a scientifically advanced grass type that will ensure that your grass stands out from the rest of the neighborhood.

For expert advice on which grass type is perfect for your area, check with your local agricultural office. They will know exactly what issues you will likely be dealing with and can provide accurate advice on grass species locally.

Furthermore, check with the National Turfgrass Evaluation Program (NTEP) to hone in on exactly what type of grass species is perfect for your area. NTEP will have information on the newest available grass types. Before I recommend any type of grass species to friends located in a different region of the county, I always check with the NTEP before giving my advice. You can access them at www.ntep. org.

WARM CLIMATE GRASS OPTIONS

If you are located in the southern parts of the United States you will be limited to warm-climate grass options. If you are located just north of the warm climate area, in the transition zone, you can also choose warm climate grass options. These grasses thrive in hot conditions where grasses that are designated for cold areas would wilt and die.

Warm-climate grass species grow quickly during the hot summer months but often go dormant during the winter months even if it isn't that cold. If there is a significant cold spell, these warm-climate grasses can even die off completely. Oftentimes, people with warm-climate grass will overseed their lawn with cold-climate grass species before winter begins so their lawn remains green all year long.

On the positive side, warm-climate grasses can grow in rocky, low-nutrient soil and clay, while cold-climate grasses require better soil and more fertilizer. The most common warm climate grasses include Bermuda grass, Zoysia grass,

11

Saint Augustine grass, Centipede grass, Buffalo grass, and Bahia grass.

Bermuda Grass

Bermuda grass is a warm-climate grass that is commonly found in the southeastern United States. This type of grass is known for its ability to withstand high temperatures and is fairly drought-tolerant. Bermuda grass is a popular choice for those who want a low-maintenance lawn.

Bermuda grass is used in locations with high foot traffic such as golf courses, sporting events, and lawns. Typically, the best time to plant Bermuda grass is in the early summer season.

Bermuda grass germinates in 7 to 15 days. Bermuda grass comes in Tifway, Tifgreen, Yuma, and Sundevil varieties. Bermuda grass is typically cut at a height of 1/2 to 1 inch. Bermuda grass should be fertilized at around 4 pounds per 1,000 square feet of area per year.

Pros Of Bermuda Grass

Bermuda grass is the gold standard in the southeast, as it requires very little maintenance, can be mowed quite low, and grows in just about any soil type. Additionally, Bermuda grass can tolerate salt, along with possessing deep, anchoring roots that make it tolerant to drought and high heat.

Cons Of Bermuda Grass

Bermuda grass starts going dormant when temperatures reach between 50°F and 60°F. When this happens, the grass quickly turns brown. Bermuda grass requires direct sunlight and does not grow well in shady areas.

Zoysia Grass

Zoysia grass is a warm-climate grass that is native to Asia. This type of grass is known for its thick, dense blades of grass. Zoysia grass is a popular choice for those who want a lawn that has a high level of curb appeal. Zoysia grass looks amazing once it has filled in completely, but that usually takes a full 3 seasons so it requires patience. Zoysia grass is often used on golf courses and lawns.

Zoysia grass germinates in 10 to 14 days. Varieties of Zoysia grass include Meyer, Emerald, Victoria, De Anza, and El Toro. Zoysia grass is generally cut at a height of 1 1/2 inches to 2 inches. Zoysia grass should be fertilized at around 3 pounds per 1,000 square feet of area per year.

Pros Of Zoysia Grass

The main pro of Zoysia grass is how beautiful it looks once it has filled in completely. Zoysia grass is also resistant to drought and doesn't need to be mowed as much as other grass types.

Cons Of Zoysia Grass

The main cons of Zoysia grass are how slowly it grows and that it must be planted by plugs, not seeds. Zoysia grass also turns brown earlier than other grass types in the fall and doesn't turn green quickly in the spring. Typically, Zoysia grass grows best in an area that doesn't receive much foot traffic, but if you do end up walking on it, it may be too prickly for bare feet.

Saint Augustine Grass

Saint Augustine grass is a warm-climate turfgrass that is popular in the southern United States. Often referred to as Buffalo grass, it is in fact, a different species. Saint Augustine grass is a popular choice for residential lawns, parks, and golf course roughs. It has a medium to fine texture and forms a dense, low-growing turf.

Saint Augustine grass germinates in 11 to 14 days. Some varieties of Saint Augustine grass include Floratine, Seville, DelMar, and Floratam. Saint Augustine grass should be mowed to a height of 1 1/2 inches to 2 1/2 inches to keep weeds away and limit thatch buildup. Saint Augustine grass is generally cut at a height of 1 3/4 inches to 3 inches. Saint Augustine grass should be fertilized at around 5 pounds per 1,000 square feet of area per year.

Pros Of Saint Augustine Grass

Saint Augustine is a tough grass that can handle heavy foot traffic and extreme heat as well as high humidity. Saint Augustine grass has a high tolerance for salt, making it a good choice for coastal areas. It also has decent resistance to pests and diseases. This grass has a deep green color and a high tolerance for shade.

Cons Of Saint Augustine Grass

Saint Augustine grass is not very tolerant to the cold and has to be mowed frequently, along with consistent watering, and fertilization. In the end, Saint Augustine grass is not all that appealing to look at even if it is properly maintained.

Centipede Grass

Centipede grass is a type of grass that is popular in the southern United States that grows best in temperatures between 75°F and 95°F. This grass is not recommended for areas that are subject to high foot traffic, such as play areas or sports fields.

Centipede grass germinates in 7 to 15 days. Some varieties of Centipede grass include Tiblair, Centennial, and Oaklawn. Centipede grass should be mowed to a height of 1 inch to 2 inches. Centipede grass should be fertilized at around 1 pound per 1,000 square feet of area per year.

Pros Of Centipede Grass

Centipede grass is a slow-growing grass, so it does not need to be mowed as often as other types of grass. This grass is known for its low maintenance requirements and its ability to tolerate heat and drought. Centipede grass is a good choice for lawns that are not heavily used, such as those in residential areas. Centipede grass is a low-maintenance grass that does not require much fertilizer or water.

Cons Of Centipede Grass

This grass is not recommended for areas that are subject to high traffic, such as play areas or sports fields. Centipede grass requires a lot of water so an irrigation system is recommended. Centipede grass does not enjoy cold weather and does not grow well in salty soil.

Buffalo Grass

Buffalo grass is the perfect southern turfgrass for anyone who doesn't want to perform a lot of maintenance. Buffalo grass germinates in 11 to 14 days. Some varieties of Buffalo grass include Prairie, Texoka, and 609. Buffalo grass should be mowed to a height of 2 inches to 3 inches. Buffalo grass should be fertilized at around 1 pound per 1,000 square feet of area per year.

Pros Of Buffalo Grass

After planting Buffalo grass it can be left alone, as it doesn't require much fertilizer, water, or consistent mowing. In fact, Buffalo grass can be allowed to grow up to 10 inches long but looks ideal when it is cut shorter. Buffalo grass is also quite tolerant to heat.

Cons Of Buffalo Grass

Buffalo grass turns brown before other grass types and does not like to be planted in a shady area.

Bahia Grass

Bahia grass was once considered only acceptable for fields, but many are choosing it for their lawns, as it requires limited maintenance. Bahia grass grows quickly and densely, not allowing weeds to gain a foothold. Typically, Bahia grass is used on golf courses and lawns. Bahia grass is generally cut at a height of 2 inches. Bahia grass should be fertilized at around 3 pounds per 1,000 square feet of area per year.

Bahia grass germinates in 8 to 15 days. Some varieties of Bahia grass include Paraguay, Pensacola, and Argentine.

Pros Of Bahia Grass

Bahia grass does well in the shade and has a deep root system that grows well in nearly any type of soil, including sand. Bahia grass doesn't need much water to maintain hydration so it doesn't typically require irrigation. Bahia grass is perfect for the coastline, as it reduces erosion and can tolerate salty conditions.

Cons Of Bahia Grass

Bahia grass is sharp to the touch and requires consistent mowing for decent curb appeal.

17

Warm-Climate Grass Characteristics

Choosing your warm climate grass should focus on what characteristics you want for your lawn.

As far as texture, the finest options include Buffalo grass and Bermuda grass. In the middle ground are Bahia grass, Centipede grass, and Zoysia grass. The coarsest option is Saint Augustine grass.

Consider your climate when choosing the best grass species to plant. All warm-climate grass options have excellent heat tolerance. However, in regards to cold tolerance, the grass species with the most resistance to cold is Buffalo grass, followed by Zoysia grass. In the middle of the pack is Bermuda grass and the grass types with the lowest cold tolerance include Bahia grass, Saint Augustine grass, and Centipede grass.

Consider the amount of precipitation you receive when choosing the right grass species. Bermuda grass, Buffalo grass, and Zoysia grass all have the highest drought tolerance. Bahia grass and Saint Augustine grass fall right in the middle of the pack and Centipede grass has the lowest drought tolerance.

If there are going to be shady spots that cover your lawn, consider planting Zoysia grass or Saint Augustine grass, as they have the highest shade tolerance. Centipede grass and Bahia grass are also shade-tolerant options. The grasses with the lowest shade tolerance include Buffalo grass and Bermuda grass.

How high do you want to mow your lawn? If you prefer a relatively long-cut height, Bahia grass and Saint Augustine grass are the two best choices. Buffalo grass and Bermuda grass can also be cut a little bit higher than Zoysia grass.

Consider the amount of fertilizer you will have to put on your lawn. If you are looking to apply the least amount of fertilizer, consider Bahia grass or Centipede grass. Buffalo grass and Zoysia grass are also quite low in fertilizer requirements. Both Saint Augustine grass and Bermuda grass prefer high amounts of fertilizer.

Anyone with property near the coast should consider the salt content of their soil and choose a grass species like Zoysia grass, Bermuda grass, Saint Augustine grass, or Buffalo grass if their soil is saline. Both Centipede grass and Bahia grass don't do well in salty soil.

The grasses that have the lowest disease issues include Bahia grass, Buffalo grass, and Centipede grass. Zoysia grass is more susceptible to diseases while Saint Augustine grass has the highest potential for developing diseases.

If you want to trample your lawn down on a regular basis, Bermuda grass and Zoysia grass have the highest wear resistance. Centipede grass has the lowest wear resistance while Saint Augustine grass, Bahia grass, and Buffalo grass all fall right in the middle of the pack.

After overusing your lawn, Saint Augustine grass, Bermuda grass, and Bahia grass recover the quickest, while Centipede grass and Zoysia grass recover the slowest.

If you want your lawn to be established as quickly as possible, choose Bermuda grass. If you have time and are willing to wait for your lawn to fill in, Centipede grass, Zoysia grass, Bahia grass, Buffalo grass, and Saint Augustine grass are all viable options.

Thatch buildup is fastest with Bermuda grass, Zoysia grass, and Saint Augustine grass. On the other hand, Bahia grass and Centipede grass have the lowest amount of thatch buildup.

Overall maintenance levels are highest with Bermuda grass and Saint Augustine grass. Normal maintenance is required for Zoysia grass. The least amount of maintenance corresponds with Bahia grass, Buffalo grass, and Centipede grass.

COLD-CLIMATE GRASS OPTIONS

Anyone located in the northern half of the United States will be limited to cold-climate grass options. Cold-climate grasses enjoy the spring and fall when temperatures hover between 60°F and 70°F. During this time fertilization, watering, and mowing your lawn consistently make the greatest impact on your yard. Anytime daytime temperatures exceed 90°F for an extended period of time, cold climate grass types suffer and often end up going dormant.

People in the transition zone can also grow cold climate grasses. Fortunately, cold climate grasses are some of the most beautiful grass types in the world, as they are extremely soft, fill in well, and display a beautiful, dark green color when properly maintained. The most common cold-climate grass options include Kentucky Bluegrass, Tall Fescue, Perennial Ryegrass, Fine Fescue, and Creeping Bentgrass.

Kentucky Bluegrass

Kentucky Bluegrass is a cool-climate grass that is native to Europe. This type of grass is known for its beautiful blue-green color. Kentucky Bluegrass is a popular choice for those who don't mind a high-maintenance lawn. Kentucky Bluegrass is the golden standard that all other grass types have to try to live up to. This grass is used for golf fairways, sporting events, and high-traffic lawns.

Kentucky Bluegrass germinates in 14 to 28 days. Kentucky Bluegrass comes in a number of varieties including Adelphi, Eclipse, Midnight, Touchdown, and Blacksburg, to name a few. Kentucky Bluegrass is generally cut at a height of 1 3/4 inches to 3 inches. Kentucky Bluegrass should be fertilized at around 5 pounds per 1,000 square feet of area per year.

Pros Of Kentucky Bluegrass

Kentucky Bluegrass is beautiful with an extremely desirable color and a soft texture. Kentucky Bluegrass also grows densely and expands to create thick turf. This grass is quite durable, cold tolerant, and handles stress well. Kentucky Bluegrass seeds are extremely small so only 2 to 3 lbs are required to seed a 1,000-foot area.

Kentucky Bluegrass is tolerant to an extremely low cut between 1/2 inch and 2 inches. However, a cut height between 2 ½ inches and 3 inches is normal. When mowed, Kentucky Bluegrass stripes well and this is why it is often used for professional sporting events like Major League Baseball.

Cons Of Kentucky Bluegrass

Kentucky Bluegrass is drought tolerant but quickly goes dormant during the hot summers, turning brown. While not necessarily harmful to the grass, a dormant lawn during the hottest summer months doesn't make for an appealing look unless it is watered consistently. Fortunately, as fall comes around, Kentucky Bluegrass quickly regains its color, as if summer didn't even happen.

If left to grow higher than about 3 inches, Kentucky Bluegrass can be susceptible to fungal issues. Additionally, since Kentucky Bluegrass grows so thick, it produces a lot of thatch that needs to be removed on a regular basis.

Kentucky Bluegrass isn't very shade tolerant and requires more water and fertilizer overall. In other words, this grass requires more general maintenance than other grass types. Finally, Kentucky Bluegrass grows extremely slowly, and can take about a year for it to completely fill in and finally look appealing.

Tall Fescue

Tall Fescue is a cool-climate grass that is commonly found in the northern United States. This type of grass is known for its tall, dense blades, and was once only considered pasture grass. However, with human intervention, new species made it softer, better looking, and more desirable. Tall Fescue is a popular choice for those who want a higher-cut lawn, with the desired cut height somewhere between 2 1/2 inches and 3 1/2 inches. Tall Fescue should be fertilized at around 4 pounds per 1,000 square feet of area per year.

Tall Fescue is used for sporting events, playgrounds, and lawns that are subject to high foot traffic.

Tall Fescue grass germinates in 7 to 14 days. Tall Fescue comes in varieties like Wrangler, Amigo, Apache, Rebel, and Tribute.

Pros Of Tall Fescue Grass

Tall Fescue grass is extremely drought tolerant, the most of any other grass type in cold climates. This is because Tall Fescue grass is taller and has a deeper root system than other grass types, thereby holding in moisture. These traits allow Tall Fescue grass to remain green during periods of drought when other grass types end up turning brown.

Tall Fescue grass also has a great color and stripes well when mowed. Tall Fescue grass is relatively tolerant to shade and requires less maintenance overall when compared to both Perennial Ryegrass and Kentucky Bluegrass.

Cons Of Tall Fescue Grass

Although new varieties of tall Fescue grass are soft to the touch, they still don't have a texture on par with Kentucky Bluegrass or perennial Ryegrass. Additionally, reel mowing tall Fescue grass doesn't create the same effect that it does on other grass types and isn't recommended.

Since tall Fescue grass holds in moisture so well, it often suffers from fungal issues, causing brown patches. Typically, basic fungicides can take care of this issue.

Finally, tall Fescue grass seeds are quite large so they require between 8 and 10 pounds to fill a 1000-foot area. Realize that you are going to have to buy more seeds to fill in the same area than you would with other grass varieties.

Perennial Ryegrass

Perennial Ryegrass is a cool-climate grass that is commonly found in the northern United States. This type of grass is known for its ability to germinate quickly and for being very wear-resistant. Perennial Ryegrass is another popular choice for those who prefer a high-maintenance lawn. Perennial Ryegrass should be fertilized at around 4 pounds per 1,000 square feet of area per year.

Oftentimes, Perennial Ryegrass is grown alongside other grass types like Kentucky Bluegrass because it grows quickly and fills in the lawn while Kentucky Bluegrass takes more time in doing so.

Perennial Ryegrass is used in sporting events and lawns, while also being used to overseed warm-climate grasses to make them look better during the winter. Perennial Ryegrass germinates in 3 to 14 days. Perennial Ryegrass comes in the varieties SR-4200, Citation II, and Manhattan II.

Pros Of Perennial Ryegrass

Perennial Ryegrass is one of the softest grass types so if you prefer to walk around barefoot on your lawn, this is the grass for you. Additionally, Perennial Ryegrass is wear resistant so it is a good option in areas that have a lot of foot traffic.

Perennial Ryegrass is also one of the darkest green grasses when compared to the other cold-climate grass types. If you want the darkest hue of green grass, look for an upper-echelon Perennial Ryegrass that is optimized for this characteristic. Since Perennial Ryegrass seeds are medium-sized, 5 to 7 lbs can cover an area of 1,000 sq feet. Perennial Ryegrass grows quickly and establishes itself far before other varieties like Kentucky Bluegrass.

Perennial Ryegrass looks best when cut somewhere between 2 inches and 3 inches. Additionally, Perennial

Ryegrass creates excellent stripes so it looks exceptional after it is mowed. Perennial Ryegrass looks even better when it is reel mowed.

Cons Of Perennial Ryegrass

Perennial Ryegrass is not very drought resistant so an irrigation system should be set up if you plant this grass. Perennial Ryegrass is also the least tolerant of high temperatures of any of the cold climate grasses and tends to brown quickly in the presence of high heat.

If Perennial Ryegrass is left to grow higher, seed heads and stalks will grow, and eventually turn brown, making for an unappealing lawn. To prevent this, it is best to keep this grass cut height on the lower end.

Perennial Ryegrass is also susceptible to fungal infections, mainly Pythium and Gray Leaf Spot. Generally, Phosphite treatments are enough to take care of fungal issues.

Fine Fescue Grass

Fine Fescue is a cool-climate grass that is commonly found in the northern United States. This type of grass is known for its ability to withstand cold temperatures and is shade-tolerant. Typically, most people only plant Fine Fescue grass in locations that are shaded, as this variety doesn't do well in direct sunlight. Fine Fescue grass germinates in 5 to 14 days. Fine Fescue should be fertilized at around 3 pounds per 1,000 square feet of area per year. Fine Fescue is generally cut at a height of 1 1/2 inches to 2 1/2 inches.

Pros Of Fine Fescue

Fine Fescue is the softest of all the grass types we discussed and requires very little maintenance. Without requiring much fertilizer or much care outside of mowing, Fine Fescue is great for shaded areas.

Once planted, the creeping varieties of Fine Fescue can spread out and fill in bare areas. Fine Fescue grass can be mowed low and is generally best at a cut height of about 2 inches.

Cons Of Fine Fescue Grass

As stated before, Fine Fescue grass does not do well in direct sunlight which is why it is only planted in shaded areas. When exposed to heat, this grass quickly goes dormant and turns brown.

Creeping Bentgrass

Creeping Bentgrass is one of my favorite grass types because we used it on the putting greens. Creeping Bentgrass is extremely unique, as it grows densely, can be cut extremely low, and has a soft texture. This is why putting greens can be cut at a height of 1/4 of an inch without scalping it. Creeping Bentgrass germinates in 6 to 10 days. Creeping Bentgrass is generally cut at a height of 1/4 inch to 3/4 of an inch.

If for some reason you want to put a putting green on your lawn, (trust me, you want to) realize that Creeping Bentgrass requires a significant amount of maintenance to keep it short, irrigated, and fertilized consistently. Typically, most homeowners don't consider Creeping Bentgrass an option for any part of their lawn, due to the maintenance it entails.

Cold-Climate Grass Characteristics

Deciding on which grass you want for your lawn should come down to specific characteristics.

As far as grass texture, Tall Fescue is the roughest, while Kentucky Bluegrass and Perennial Ryegrass are a bit finer.

Consider your climate, if it gets extremely hot in the summertime, plant Tall Fescue, as it has the highest heat tolerance. Kentucky Bluegrass has some heat tolerance characteristics, while Perennial Ryegrass doesn't do well in the heat.

On the other hand, the grass that has the highest cold tolerance is Creeping Bentgrass. Kentucky Bluegrass is right in the middle of the pack while Tall Fescue and Perennial Ryegrass have the lowest tolerance to the cold.

If you live in a dry climate, consider planting Tall Fescue, as it has the highest drought tolerance. After that, Kentucky Bluegrass and Perennial Ryegrass are lower on the scale of drought tolerance, while Creeping Bentgrass is the lowest, as it requires a constant supply of water.

Consider where you are going to be planting your lawn. If there are many areas that are going to be shaded, Fine Fescue is the best option. After that, Tall Fescue has a relatively high shade tolerance. Perennial Ryegrass and Creeping Bentgrass are right in the middle of the shade tolerance spectrum, while Kentucky Bluegrass is not tolerant of shady conditions at all.

How high or low do you want to mow your grass? If you prefer a higher cut height, Tall Fescue and Fine Fescue are the go-to options. Perennial Ryegrass and Kentucky Bluegrass can also be cut a bit higher if desired. On the other end of the spectrum, Creeping Bentgrass must be cut extremely low.

When considering which type of grass seed to plant, think about fertilizer requirements. Creeping Bentgrass requires the most fertilizer while Kentucky Bluegrass and Perennial Ryegrass also prefer a steady diet of fertilizer. On the other hand, Tall Fescue and Fine Fescue require the least fertilizer overall.

Grass types that have the highest resistance to diseases include Tall Fescue first, Kentucky Bluegrass next, and Perennial Ryegrass third. Creeping Bentgrass has the highest potential for developing diseases.

If you are located near the ocean or somewhere else that has salty soil, plant a grass species like Tall Fescue which has the highest salt tolerance. Perennial Ryegrass is also somewhat tolerant to salt, but Kentucky Bluegrass and Fine Fescue don't grow well in salty soils.

Decide how you are going to use your lawn and if you plan to throw lots of parties and daily kickball games you are going to want a wear-resistant grass strain. Tall Fescue has the highest wear resistance. On the other end of the spectrum, Perennial Ryegrass, Kentucky Bluegrass, and Fine Fescue don't offer much wear resistance. At the very lowest end of the spectrum of wear resistance sits Creeping Bentgrass which is one reason why golf courses insist that you don't drive the golf cart onto the greens.

If your lawn receives a lot of foot traffic after a weekend party, Kentucky Bluegrass and Creeping Bentgrass are the fastest to recover from that experience. After that, Tall

Fescue and Perennial Ryegrass spring back, but at a slower rate. The slowest grass type to recover from overuse is Fine Fescue.

If your main focus is on developing your lawn in the shortest amount of time, Perennial Ryegrass germinates the quickest and becomes established in no time. Both Tall Fescue and Fine Fescue are also quick to develop. On the other end of the spectrum, Kentucky Bluegrass is extremely slow to germinate and develop into a dense lawn.

Another aspect to consider when deciding on which grass seed to buy is how much thatch each variety produces. The lowest thatch buildup comes from Tall Fescue and Perennial Ryegrass. After that, Kentucky Bluegrass and Fine Fescue are in the middle of the range in regards to thatch buildup. On the high end of the range, Creeping Bentgrass quickly builds up thatch.

How much maintenance do you want to do on your lawn? The highest maintenance grass type is Creeping Bentgrass. The lowest maintenance grass type is Tall Fescue. In the middle of the pack, Kentucky Bluegrass, Perennial Ryegrass, and Fine Fescue require moderate amounts of maintenance for a decent-looking lawn.

The Crucial Decision - What Grass Type Will You Plant?

As you can see, if you are located in a cold climate or in the transition zone, typically your options include Perennial Ryegrass, Kentucky Bluegrass, Tall Fescue grass for sunny areas, and Fine Fescue grass for shaded areas. Each of these grass types has its own pros and cons, but all are extremely desirable generally speaking.

Oftentimes, homeowners choose a blend which means a number of different varieties of one specific species of grass.

Other times, a mix is the best option, meaning that multiple different grass species are all contained in one bag of seeds. For instance, if you are planting cool climate grass, a mix of Kentucky Bluegrass, Perennial Ryegrass, and multiple varieties of Fescue are all contained in the same bag.

Typically, choosing a blend or a mix is the most common option instead of just planting one specific variety of grass seeds so you get the pros of each type of grass while minimizing the cons.

For the best results, work with your local agricultural office and the NTEP that were mentioned earlier to hone in on the perfect grass seeds for your lawn.

BASIC LAWN CARE TERMINOLOGY

If you are an absolute beginner in lawn care maintenance, there are some terms that you need to get familiar with. If you are already experienced with lawn maintenance, you may want to skip ahead to the next chapter.

Dethatching

The buildup of thatch is inevitable, but there are certain procedures to follow to reduce the formation of thatch. First, water your lawn thoroughly, yet infrequently so the roots grow deeply and don't only occupy the soil surface. Second, don't overfertilize your lawn, as it leads to excessive growth and thatch buildup. Third, mow your lawn frequently and don't cut off more than a third of your lawn's length, as excessive grass clippings don't break down quickly, leading to thatch buildup.

Overusing pesticides kill off microorganisms in the soil that break down thatch. Soil pH that isn't near neutral and compacted soil makes it hard to break down thatch. Soil that contains significant quantities of clay contributes to compaction and therefore, results in thatch build-up. Certain grass types like Zoysia grass, Bermuda grass, and Kentucky Bluegrass are most susceptible to thatch buildup.

Dethatching refers to the process of removing dead grass and debris from the lawn so it looks better, is easier to mow, and makes overseeding the lawn more efficient. After removing dead grass, existing grass has a chance to thicken up and fill in the space left behind.

Every lawn has some thatch and a small amount actually improves the health of the grass, as it holds in moisture and improves wear resistance.

However, significant thatch build-up, as defined by 1/2 inch or more, prevents water from absorbing into the soil and can result in browning grass. Removing thatch on a regular basis, at least once a year, is the key to making your lawn look its best.

If you want to dethatch your entire lawn, it is best to rent a power rake or vertical mower, as the reels spin through your grass and pull out the thatch. If you are only dethatching a small area, a dethatching rake should do the job, but it certainly qualifies as manual labor so consider yourself warned.

After running a dethatching machine over your yard, go back with a dethatching rake and remove any excess thatch that was left behind.

Typically, after dethatching, it makes sense to core aerate to increase water absorption into the soil and facilitate new grass growth.

Now, remove all the thatch and cores, ideally with a lawn-mower and bag attachment. Since the process of dethatching and core aeration is stressful on your lawn, immediately add fertilizer and water it to facilitate new growth.

Core Aeration

Core aeration involves pulling out cores of grass and soil so more air and nutrients can enter into the soil. Core aeration increases the seed and soil contact which is why this process is generally used before overseeding.

A gas-powered core aeration machine makes quick work out of this process. Simply run it over your lawn and it will pull out cores of soil, thereby de-compacting the soil and improving root health. Typically, punch holes evenly around 3 inches apart and 3 inches deep over your entire lawn.

Ideally, run the core aerator in one direction first and then go back over your lawn at a 90° angle, punching out cores again. The best time to core aerate is when the soil is moist but not overly wet and definitely not when dry. There is another option that uses spikes to punch holes into your lawn, but core aerating is far more effective.

Core aerating allows your grass to breathe, as the roots have better access to air, water, and nutrients. Additionally, core aerating creates a better environment for microorganisms that will in turn break down thatch. Ideally, perform the process of core aerating your lawn at least once a year. If you have high levels of clay in your soil, you will want to core aerate more often to reduce soil compaction.

It is best to leave the cores scattered all over your lawn, as they will quickly break down within weeks. If of course, you don't want to look at them, you can either rake them up or run your lawnmower over them with the bag attachment to pick them up.

In any case, if you don't have much thatch to deal with, you can get away with simply core aerating your lawn and not having to dethatch as well.

When core aerating, focus on the areas that are prone to foot traffic, as the soil will be more compacted in these regions. Also, core aerating in places where water puddles up will encourage better drainage. If you apply water and it quickly runs off your lawn after only a bit of irrigation, core aeration will open up your lawn and encourage the water to seep into your soil.

Overseeding

After a lawn is established but requires further grass to fill it in completely, grass seeds are applied over the lawn, a process known as overseeding. Overseeding is typically applied in springtime or in the fall time to the existing lawn. If you are overseeding your lawn, you cannot use a pre-emergent herbicide that would typically be applied in the spring.

Overseeding is ideal when there aren't many weeds, but the lawn hasn't filled in completely. Overseeding in a cool climate is best done in the fall. Overseeding in a warm climate with a warm climate grass is best in the spring. However, overseeding in a warm climate with a cold climate grass is best done in the fall to maintain the lawn's green color throughout winter.

Before overseeding your lawn, mow it quite a bit lower than normal, almost to the point of scalping it, to increase the available area for new seeds to germinate and grow. The idea is that grass seeds should come in contact with the soil, not the grass above it.

After mowing the lawn, remove the clippings instead of letting them remain on the lawn. Again, removing excess grass will increase the probability of seed and soil contact.

Now, rake the entire lawn at the very least, or better yet, dethatch the lawn to remove dead grass that has accumulated over time. Again, the idea is the same, removing excess thatch allows seeds to get down into the soil easier. After dethatching, performing core aeration is a good idea to counteract compacted soil.

Follow the seeding rate on the side of the bag recommended for overseeding your lawn. Generally, overseeding requires around three times the amount of seeds than seeding on bare soil does. The reason more seeds are required when overseeding is that many of those seeds won't reach the soil and germinate. By applying more seeds, seed and soil contact increases.

After overseeding your lawn, roll it with a push roller to compact the seeds down into the soil, increasing the probability of germination.

Now, apply starter fertilizer throughout the entire lawn and cover the lawn with a thin layer of mulch, like straw, to protect the developing seeds.

As with any seeding project, it is important to water your lawn multiple times a day initially to encourage germination and allow seedlings to develop.

As soon as the new grass has grown high enough that it can be cut down to the desired cut height, mow your lawn.

Going forward, your lawn will continue to thicken up and develop into compact turf.

Pre-emergent

Pre-emergent refers to an herbicide that is applied before weeds like crabgrass, foxtail, and goosegrass develop in the spring. Pre-emergents function by killing off the root system of developing weeds.

Post-emergent

A post-emergent refers to an herbicide that is applied after weeds are already present. Typically, post-emergent herbicides are less effective than pre-emergent herbicides, as they have to kill the weeds after they are already established.

Top Dressing

Top dressing is the process of applying a layer of straw, hydromulch, or wood fiber over germinating grass seeds to protect them and hold onto moisture.

Reel Mower

A reel mower is a specific type of lawnmower that uses reel blades instead of the typical rotary cutting blades found on most gas-powered lawnmowers. Reel mowers allow one to cut the grass lower, more evenly, and provide a better look overall.

Now that we have that out of the way, let's discuss the process of planting your lawn from scratch.

CHAPTER 2 - PLANTING YOUR LAWN FROM SEED

While it is a good idea to order the grass seeds you want early to ensure you have them ready to go, you can't just start tossing seeds around your barren land and hope they germinate into a thick, lush lawn. Let's take a look at the step-by-step process of planting your lawn and discuss the ideal times of the year to put this plan into motion.

I am going to assume that you are starting from the very beginning and are looking at a yard full of dirt with plans to seed your lawn. Later, we will focus more on renovating your lawn and other aspects of lawn care.

Your Lawn Will Only Be As Good As The Soil Supporting It

I know it's not glamorous, but just before planting your lawn is the most ideal time to get your soil tested. With this information, you can customize your approach to lawn care and have the best lawn from a scientific standpoint. If you don't want to test your soil, going forward, everything you do will just be a guess.

Hand Testing Your Soil Composition

One thing you can do without a professional soil test is to determine what your soil is made out of. First, take a handful of soil and squeeze it. As you unclasp your hand, take a look at the soil to determine its composition.

If the soil is sandy, it will break apart quickly. If your soil contains high quantities of clay, you'll be left with a ball of soil in your hand that doesn't break up. If your soil is loamy, it will end up compacting in your fist, but break apart once you touch it. Knowing the composition of your soil makes it easier to select the proper grass type for your lawn.

A Professional Soil Analysis

A soil test will determine the pH, mineral levels, organic matter, and overall composition of the soil. If one of these factors needs some adjustments, now is the time to do it, before planting grass.

Additionally, knowing the exact composition of your soil and modifying it now will likely save you money over the long term.

Avoid using basic home soil test kits that you can find nearly anywhere, that only indicate pH level. While this information is helpful, we require a broad overview of the entire soil so a more detailed soil test is necessary.

A detailed soil test takes some time, generally at least a few weeks and sometimes as long as a month. For this reason, submit your soil sample at least a month before you plan to plant your lawn so you can make adjustments beforehand.

Taking A Soil Sample

The most efficient way to take a soil sample is to use a soil probe that digs in and pulls out a core of around 6 inches of soil. However, there are other techniques like using a spade or shovel to obtain a soil sample.

First, put on a pair of nitrile or latex gloves so you don't contaminate the soil sample you are going to take. Ideally, pull a core soil sample from multiple locations across the yard, something like 15 different cores. Then, mix all of this soil together in a clean bucket, while removing thatch and roots so there is only soil resting in the bottom.

At this point, mix together all the soil and send off a sample for analysis to any soil analytical company you choose. I personally use a company called Waypoint Labs, as they are located all across the country.

After receiving the results of a soil sample back that contain graphs and recommendations, it's easy to make adjustments.

Soil pH

One of the most important aspects of a soil sample is the pH. Ideally, your soil should be between a pH of 6.5 and 7.0. If your pH is over 7.0, the way to bring it down is with an application of granulated ammonium sulfate. If your pH is below 6.5, applying lime in pellet form will push it higher. Avoid using powder pH enhancers, as a little bit often pushes the pH too far in one direction.

The amount of lime or sulfur you will need to add to change the pH of your soil depends on the composition of your soil. Sandy soil requires less of either, loam soil a moderate amount, and clay soil requires the most lime or sulfur to change the pH.

Obtaining soil in the optimal pH range will ensure optimal growth and increase the bioavailability of fertilizer.

Macronutrients

The next thing to look at is the macro analysis of nutrients like nitrogen, phosphorus, and potassium. If low in any of these macronutrients, adjust your soil accordingly. Correcting imbalances, specifically phosphorus and potassium levels, is extremely important now before planting seeds, as these two minerals are essential for proper root development. Nitrogen, while extremely important for foliage development, takes on a more significant role after the root system has developed.

Oftentimes, people who apply fertilizer blind will develop an imbalance that can lock out other nutrients, resulting in a subpar lawn.

Micronutrients

A close look at the micronutrients like calcium, magnesium, and iron can provide valuable information. If any of these minerals are lacking, add them back into the soil.

Soluble Salts

Your soil test will also indicate how much salt is in your soil. Generally, only people located close to the ocean or other regions with high quantities of salt may have an issue with high salinity.

If you have excess salt in your soil, you can add gypsum, a calcium-rich material that helps pull sodium from the soil when it is watered.

Organic Matter

Taking a look at the organic matter present in your soil indicates how fertile it is. If this is low, organic matter like compost, manure, and peat moss can be added to the soil. Ideally, spread organic compost throughout your yard, especially if you have sandy soil to enhance the nutrient content and retain moisture. This organic material will contribute to a lawn that has beneficial microorganisms and worms.

If you only have a small area to cover, you can buy compost in bags, but if you are adding it to your entire lawn, it is best to purchase it by the dump truckload. Additionally, compost purchased in bulk will be less expensive and pay off big time when your lawn starts to fill in.

Proper Topsoil Depth

For a spectacular lawn, you will need at least 7 inches of topsoil to support the grass above. Measure your topsoil throughout your yard and if it is not at least 7 inches deep, add more topsoil to increase the depth.

If you have to add more topsoil to your yard, purchase it by load and have it delivered to you instead of purchasing it bag by bag. Overall, it will cost far less to buy a dump truck full of topsoil than it will to buy individual bags of topsoil.

After adding sufficient topsoil, rototill it into the existing soil in preparation for adding necessary nutrients back in after soil test results come back. If you don't plan on having a garden, renting a rototiller instead of buying it makes the most sense, as you shouldn't have to use it again once your lawn is set. Then, after supplementing the amendments into the soil with a spreader, level out the yard in preparation for planting seeds.

Using Your Soil Analysis To Perfect Your Soil

Nearly everyone who has a perfect lawn takes a soil sample before planting their lawn and again every 2 or 3 years so they know exactly how to improve their lawn. While many people can still have an excellent lawn even if they are flying blind, it makes sense to get a soil sample for obvious reasons.

PLANTING YOUR COLD CLIMATE LAWN IN THE EARLY FALL AND WARM CLIMATE LAWN IN THE LATE SPRING

By far, the best time to plant your cold climate lawn is in the fall time so it has a chance to germinate and fill in before winter. The main advantage of planting your lawn in the fall is that soil temperatures are still high, ensuring ideal seed germination rates. Specifically, aim to plant your lawn when soil temperatures are between 60°F and 75°F. While your lawn likely won't be perfect when spring comes around, you can overseed at that time to fill in bare spots.

If you are located in the south or transition zone and want to plant warm climate grass types, the best time to do so is in the late spring, right before summer, when soil temperatures are between 75°F and 85°F, as these species germinate well when soil temperatures are high.

Look at your 7-day weather forecast and choose a time to plant your lawn when there isn't any extreme weather coming in. While a little rain is beneficial, a torrential downpour or extremely windy conditions will displace seeds and result in uneven growth.

Now you know when is the best time to plant your grass seeds. However, you can't just throw seeds everywhere and expect the best results, as there is some preparation work to do before planting your lawn.

Sourcing Ideal Grass Seeds

Secure the lawn seed you want now to ensure there is an adequate supply and you have it on hand, ready to go when needed. In some areas, there are supply chain issues when it comes to securing lawn seed so ensure it is available and obtain it now before it is all sold out.

As stated before, search for ideal lawn seeds that have optimal genetics and be willing to spend the extra money to buy these seeds. There is no substitute for genetics and if you want the best lawn imaginable you must have the best lawn genetics first and foremost. Generally, you won't find these seeds at your local big box store so go directly to your local horticulture store or look online.

After entering your local lawn and garden center, take out your magnifying glass and be ready to read the side of each lawn seed label. At this point, you should already know exactly what type of lawn seed you are looking for so that should immediately narrow down your search. If you already know the variety of the specific seed species you want, look directly for these options. For instance, if you know you want Adelphi Kentucky Bluegrass seeds, this will narrow down your search to a minimum.

Thanks to The Federal Seed Act of 1936, labeling on bags of seed is detailed and uniform across the entire country. On the lawn seed label, you will see the germination percentage, pure seed percentage, weed seed percentage, noxious weed seed percentage, other crops' seed percentage, inert matter percentage, the origin where it was grown, manufacture information, and the date it was packaged.

Look specifically for a lawn seed that has a germination percentage that is greater than 75%, full of pure seeds only, has less than 1% weed seeds, has other crop seeds that are near zero, has zero noxious weed seeds, inert matter below 1%, and is sold by a reputable manufacturer that was packaged recently.

If you are willing to spend the money on certified seeds that have near zero weeds you'll immediately notice the difference after germination. Certified seeds with zero weeds germinate into a full lawn quickly and reduce the number of weeds you will have to deal with later.

Ensure that you buy enough seeds so you can fill out your entire lawn and have some left over. The best way to do that is to measure your property and get your square footage. This should be relatively easy with a soft tape measure or even better, a rolling tape measure wheel.

Always buy more seeds than necessary because there will likely be bare spots that you will have to fill in at a later date and it is best to have the same seeds available so the lawn looks uniform.

Realize that some types of grass like Kentucky Bluegrass only require between 2 and 3 lbs to fill in a 1,000 ft area, while grass like Tall Fescue requires between 8 and 10 lb to fill in the same area.

Installing An Irrigation System

While not completely necessary, people who want to install an irrigation system should do so now so everything is in the soil and ready to go before it is leveled out. When designing an irrigation system, be sure that the water will be able to touch all areas of the property so there are no dry bare spots, ensuring the grass grows evenly.

Leveling Out Your Landscape

Before planting seeds and while waiting for the soil analysis to return, it is time to level out the soil so lawn care is more enjoyable going forward. Since you will be adding topsoil during the leveling process, it makes it easy to add nutrients back into the soil after the soil lab test returns. The ideal time to start leveling out your yard is when the soil is a bit moist, but not overly wet so it is easy to move around, yet stays in place when set.

When leveling out your lawn, it is the perfect time to form a gradient to force water away from your house, reducing the potential for foundational problems later. Any downgradient will work, but the general recommendation is that the yard should drop 2 ft for every 100 feet in distance away from the house.

Before laying any topsoil down, scout out the entire yard and remove any big rocks and other debris that is present. Having to run your lawnmower over rocks, bumps, and grooves isn't that much fun. Furthermore, a lawn that isn't leveled out isn't going to appear as nice as one that is completely smooth.

While you can take a leveling rake and do all the work manually, most people either buy or rent a four-wheeler and add a leveling hitch to the back. Then, drive all over your property leveling the dirt out until it is ready to go.

If you don't feel up to the task of leveling out your soil, contract out the work to a professional, as they have the machinery to quickly handle the job and ensure your soil is entirely level before planting grass seeds. Since it is difficult to level your yard after your lawn is already set, spend the time, energy, and money initially so you don't have to worry about it for years to come.

Planting Your Seeds

When planting seeds, think scientifically and apply the correct amount of seeds to the area to ensure a thick, lush grass, but don't overseed the area. On the side of a bag of grass seeds it will display the proper rate to seed your lawn so follow that strictly. Ideally, measure out the seeds on a scale to ensure exactness.

If you have never seeded a lawn before, start out by measuring out a small area like a 100 ft region, and practice seeding here, ensuring that you have spread the seed evenly throughout the area. The best way to do that is to start out slowly and walk in random directions distributing the seeds with the spreader until the entire area is adequately covered with seeds. At that point, with an understanding of how to properly seed that area, expand out to the rest of the property and seed it completely.

One of the most crucial tools you will need for spreading fertilizer and planting your seeds is a spreader. Think of buying a spreader as an investment so look for a nice spreader now and don't try to save a couple of bucks by only renting this unit.

A spreader will enable you to dial in the seeding rate so simply follow the seeding rate that is listed on the side of the bag of grass seeds. While you can use a hand seeder, investing in a drop spreader or a rotary spreader is going to make your life a lot easier.

Kill Two Birds With One Stone - Add Starter Fertilizer And Weed Killer Together

At this point, spread starter fertilizer over the entire property and a weed killer like mesotrione, under the brand name Tenacity, that kills certain weeds and doesn't affect grass seeds. While Tenacity doesn't kill all weeds, it does a good job at taking care of most weeds so you won't have to deal with weeds as much in the future.

Some starter fertilizers contain Tenacity in them so you can just spread a granular fertilizer and weed-killer product in one fell swoop. If you want, you can purchase both products separately, apply the starter fertilizer and then apply Tenacity after that.

If you ended up planting cheap grass seeds that have a large percentage of weeds and specifically crabgrass, there

47

is a solution. Immediately apply the pre-emergent herbicide Tenacity when you plant your seeds.

Rake In The Grass Seeds

Now, take a rake and mix the grass seeds into the soil to ensure the highest amount of soil contact. Any kind of rake should be sufficient, but a metal rake will make the overall process easier.

Roll In The Seeds

Now, take a push roller and roll the seeds into the soil to ensure ideal seed-soil contact. Since most people don't have a roller on hand, renting one is usually the most common option. The soil roller doesn't have to be extremely heavy, but heavy enough to compact the seeds into the soil.

Applying Top Dressing To The Yard

Apply a top dressing to the yard to maintain soil moisture and protect the seeds from predators like birds. Typically, most people use straw as a top dressing, as it works just fine, but there are other more modern-day options like hydromulch and wood pulp. In any case, any top dressing options fit the bill and should give the grass the protection and moisture it needs for the seeds to germinate quickly.

When applying the top dressing, don't go overboard, only add 1/4 inch of material or less so you don't inhibit the growth of newly forming plants.

Watering Your Newly Forming Lawn

Watering your lawn is the most important step by far, as all the hard work you have done up to this point is dependent on proper moisture. The goal is to ensure that the soil is constantly moist so the seeds never have a chance to dry out and can quickly grow roots.

Immediately after adding the top dressing, it is time to start watering the yard so all the newly planted seeds will begin to germinate together. After this initial watering, the yard must remain moist at all times, especially during the first crucial two weeks of growth.

Ideally, start out by gently watering the soil 5 times a day until the seeds begin to germinate. One thing I see with beginners is that they overwater their seeds, resulting in puddles everywhere which lead to runoff. Since the grass root system hasn't developed yet, all 7 inches of topsoil don't need to be saturated in water. The goal is to only keep the top of the soil moist to facilitate root formation.

If the soil is overwatered, it can cause seed rot, due to a disease known as Pythium blight. This disease will effectively kill off your lawn and force you to have to start the whole process all over again. Additionally, if you use too much water on your soil, it will float away, along with your newly planted seeds, so remember that moderation is the key here.

After germination, the best way to ensure that the soil is constantly moist is to water the ground two or three times a day for about 5 minutes each time. The goal is to increase the depth to which the water reaches, generally, the first 5 inches of topsoil should be moist. This will encourage root development throughout the soil and allow the lawn to thicken up quickly.

Adjust your watering schedule with the weather and if it is extremely hot or windy, irrigate it more to maintain constant moisture within the soil.

Generally, the best time to water your lawn is in the morning, mid-morning, and mid-afternoon. If you only have an opportunity to water your lawn twice a day, do so in the mid-morning and mid-afternoon so it remains damp all day long, but not too wet at night to avoid fungus development.

If you installed an irrigation system that was discussed earlier, this is your chance to use it to its fullest potential. If you are using a sprinkler system to keep your soil moist, ensure that it is able to cover every area of the property so there are no bare spots.

In any case, don't depend on Mother Nature to give you rain when you need it most. Have a watering system in place beforehand so you are ready to keep your soil moist at all times.

Watch Your Lawn Grow

After your seeds have started to germinate, now all you have to do is sit back, crack open your favorite beverage, and watch your lawn grow, while ensuring that it is receiving enough water. Eventually, you can water your lawn less frequently, something like twice a week, as the soil will maintain moisture, as it isn't exposed to the elements. The timeframe for this is dependent on the grass species planted and how long it takes to germinate.

Protect Your Germinating
Seeds From Damage

As your grass is just germinating, you will have to keep your kids and family dog off of the seeded area if you want it to fill in with perfection. This may be easier said than done, but this critical moment of growing your lawn requires little to no foot traffic.

Ideally, rope off the grass so everyone knows that it is off limits and set up signs that say "please keep off". During this time, if you have a dog, only allow it to enter a certain area, like the back patio so it doesn't destroy your lawn even before it starts.

Mow Your Lawn With A Manual Reel Mower

While it is counterintuitive to mow your lawn too early, it is best to start mowing 2 to 3 weeks after the grass has germinated, as the root system should be developed by that time. Generally, the grass should be around 3 inches to 4 inches in height when you first mow it.

When you mow your lawn for the first time, it is best to use a manual reel mower so it isn't overly heavy and you can pick up the mower and move it without having to make sharp corners. Ideally, be as gentle as possible, especially when going around corners so it doesn't pull out newly formed grass. If you don't have a manual reel mower, you can rent one in your area. Ideally, only cut off about an inch to avoid overstressing the newly forming lawn.

The day before mowing your lawn, stop watering it so you can mow the grass when it is dry to prevent scalping. After the grass grows back to 4 inches, mow it again so it becomes accustomed to the constant mowing that will make it look its best.

Applying Fertilizer For The Second Time

Around 4 weeks after the seeds germinated, it is time to apply fertilizer again. You can apply starter fertilizer or a regular fertilizer like 10-10-10. This second batch of fertilizer will quickly improve the lawn.

Applying A Post-Emergent Weed Killer

Now that your lawn has filled in quite a bit, it should be looking fairly decent, but there may be some unsightly weeds that took up residence. Deal with these weeds by applying post-emergent herbicide directly on them. If there aren't all that many weeds, pick them by hand. In any case, it is best to deal with these weeds now, before winter hits, so they are gone once spring begins. This will allow you to avoid having to apply a pre-emergent weed killer in spring so you can perform the process of overseeding your lawn instead.

What To Expect
When Planting A New Lawn

Ideally, don't have overly high expectations when you are planting a new lawn. Obviously, not everything will fill in completely and it won't look perfect before winter rushes in. Don't worry, you will be applying seeds again in the spring when you overseed your lawn and the goal is to have an ideal lawn in one year's time after germination.

If you follow the seasonal guidelines that I will present in chapter 5, your lawn will look excellent by the time next fall arrives.

Planting Your Lawn In The Spring

Seeding your lawn in the springtime is not ideal, and if you can wait for fall time to seed your lawn, you should. However, if you have just finished construction on your new house and need some top cover so the soil doesn't erode, you won't have much other option than to seed your lawn in the springtime.

The overall process for seeding your lawn in the springtime is similar to the fall time, although germination rates are generally slower because soil temperatures are lower. For this reason, there will likely be more bare spots and weeds.

I won't go over the entire process again, as everything is similar to seeding your lawn in the fall, but the results likely won't be as good. In any case, take care of your lawn over the summer and perform the step of overseeding your lawn during the fall time to improve it before winter time. By the time spring comes around, your lawn should be on par with what you expect and continue to improve throughout the next season.

CHAPTER 3 - SODDING, SPRIGGING AND PLUGGING

There are a number of alternatives to planting your lawn from seed including transplanting sod, sprigging, plugging, and strip sodding.

DEVELOPING YOUR LAWN WITH SOD
IN THE SPRING AND FALL

Planting sod is one of the easiest solutions to obtaining a beautiful lawn within the shortest amount of time. Obviously, the drawback of sod is the excess cost, as it costs about 30% more than using seeds.

The best time to lay sod down is nearly anytime during the spring and fall. However, don't lay sod down during the middle of the summer, as the excessive heat can hinder development. Additionally, don't lay sod down immediately before winter, as it won't have a chance to establish roots if the ground is near the freezing temperature.

What If I Missed The Window Of Opportunity To Plant Seeds? Can I Plant Sod Instead?

If you missed a perfect time to plant your lawn by seed, planting sod may still be an option, as it has a larger window of time for when it can be transplanted. For that reason, many people who are slow to act on planting seeds ultimately choose to plant sod. In this case, their procrastination should be quickly rewarded, as their lawn appears nearly finished in only a month or so. The general rule is that a lawn from sod only requires 50% of the time that a lawn from seed takes to mature.

Pros Of Sod

If you have hills on your property where grass seeds would quickly run off when irrigated, sod may be a better option. On a slope, place sod and secure it with a few stakes in the middle of the strip that will ensure it doesn't slip off before its roots anchor it into the soil.

Another advantage to sod is that any weeds below in the dirt that would have germinated are choked out by the strips of sod so the lawn should start out completely weed-free.

Prepping The Soil For Sod

Realize that your soil quality is just as important when laying down sod as it is when planting seeds. For that reason, a soil sample is still required and the proper augmentation ensures that sod will be able to root quickly and thrive in the soil it is transplanted on.

Where To Buy Sod

If you've decided to start your lawn from sod instead of seed, look around your local area for sod growers and purchase grass that was grown near you to ensure that this grass is ideal for your climate.

After measuring out the square footage of your property, always order at least 10% more sod than you think you will need to fill in your lawn, as there will be areas that will need to be cut and shaped to fit perfectly. It is better to have more sod than you need, as you always want to ensure that you can completely fill in your lawn immediately without having to order extra sod later, resulting in an uneven look.

Ideally, go to your local sod grower and order your sod around a week before you are ready to lay it down. In most cases, the sod grower should be able to cut it and deliver it within 48 hours after they harvested it. This will ensure that you are laying sod that is fresh and will quickly take root.

Realize that most sod varieties were originally grown in direct sunlight so they should be planted in areas that don't have shade. If you want sod designed for shady areas, you will have to request that specifically.

Your Sod Has Arrived, It's Time To Get Busy

As soon as you receive the sod, unroll some samples and make sure there are no weeds, pests, or diseases. Ideally, sod should be entirely grass, making it easy to start with an ideal lawn.

If you notice that the sod is already dying, this is a serious problem, as it is nearly impossible to bring it back to life after transplanting it onto your property. In a case like this, get in contact with the grower and ask for a new batch of sod.

Laying Down Sod

All the prep work regarding fertilizing, leveling, and grading your soil should be complete and as soon as you receive the sod you should quickly moisten the soil and lay the sod down. If you can't lay down the sod immediately, wet it down regularly with a garden hose to ensure that it doesn't dry out it. In any case, the sod must be laid down within 48 hours of receiving it.

Ideally, you are going to want a wheelbarrow to move the rolls of sod, a small sheet of plywood or a board to put over the sod when you need to kneel or walk on it, and a knife to cut the sod so you can fit it into the lawn. As soon as you are ready to go, start laying down the sod at one edge of your property, ideally a boundary that is completely in line. Then, set up a string guideline that will ensure you are laying the sod perfectly straight.

After laying down the first row of sod, lay down the next row staggering it in a similar fashion to building a brick wall. Every row of sod should be snug tight against the next row without overlapping so it grows in tightly without resulting in unnecessary bumps.

If you have to step on the sod you just laid, place a sheet of plywood down and use that to walk on so you don't step on the sod directly.

When laying sod on a steep gradient slope, always lay it horizontally to the gradient, not vertically, as it will be more stable that way.

As you reach the end of your property, there will likely be areas that need to be filled in more, especially around curved areas so cut out the sod as needed and lay it down.

Roll The Sod Down

As soon as the entire property has a layer of sod, roll it down with a weighted roller. When going over your lawn with a roller, do so across the rows of sod, not vertically with them. This will cause them to stretch out and fill in the gaps between each strip of sod.

Watering The Newly Transplanted Sod

As soon as your entire new lawn has been set in place, your main responsibility is to get it wet and keep it wet. Ideally, the first time you irrigate your lawn, ensure that water has penetrated into the soil of a depth of at least 4 inches. To determine this, lift up a corner of the sod, stick a screwdriver into the dirt, pull it out, and make sure it is wet.

Sufficient water will encourage root development and ensure that the sod doesn't dry out. Focus especially on irrigating the edges of your property, as these will dry out first, so they may need to be watered more often.

Continue watering your sod consistently, at least once a day for the first week. After a week, check a corner of your sod to see if the roots are starting to grow into the soil below. If so, you can water a little bit less, usually only every other day, and note the results. If the lawn appears to be responding well to being watered once every other day, keep doing so, but if it appears to be drying out, go back to watering it every day.

Continue watering the lawn every other day for another two weeks and after the third week, check a corner of your lawn. At this point, you shouldn't be able to pull back the sod, as the roots should be established.

Protecting Your Newly Transplanted Sod

After laying down your sod, avoid stepping on it, and just like when planting grass seeds, place a barrier around it and a sign that says "keep off." Additionally, ensure that your kids and dog don't walk on newly laid sod. Ideally, keep foot traffic to near zero for a couple of months after laying down the sod.

After your lawn is established and everyone including your dog is enjoying it, realize that dog urine is even worse on sod than it is on a lawn planted by seed. For this reason, keep a close eye on where your dog is urinating and water urine spots down thoroughly with a garden hose so that area doesn't turn into a dead spot.

Mowing Your Lawn After Laying Down Sod

As soon as your lawn has grown to about 3 inches or 4 inches, it is time to mow it. As with planting grass from seed, only take off about an inch to avoid overstressing your grass. Again, make sure the blades on your lawnmower are as sharp as possible so they cut the grass cleanly, without pulling on newly developing sod. Ideally, use a manual reel mower the first time you mow your lawn so you can move it easily without disturbing the grass.

SPRIGGING

The term used to refer to the stem of the grass is sprig. Sprigging is simply planting that stem into the ground and allowing roots to develop in the soil. There are a variety of warm-climate grasses that are planted by sprigging including Zoysia grass, Bermuda grass, and Saint Augustine grass. The reason for this is that the seeds these grasses produce are sterile so they need to be planted by cuttings instead.

Typically, sprigs are purchased in a bushel so you will need to know exactly how big your yard is when ordering sprigs. The process of planting sprigs is time-consuming, but the more you plant, the faster your lawn will fill out.

As with planting by seed or laying down sod, the first step is to get a soil analysis and adjust your soil accordingly so it is conducive to grass growth.

Typically, sprigs are planted in a furrow, the term used to describe a small trench. These sprigs are planted in the furrow, each about a foot apart. Use a stick to push the sprig into the ground about 2 inches deep. After that, add top-soil so only 2 inches of the stem is visible, and then use a weighted roller to compress it down.

After all these sprigs are in place, it needs to be watered twice a day for at least one or two weeks to ensure the soil is constantly moist and encourage root growth.

PLUGGING

Plugging is similar to sodding your lawn, except that plugs are generally only a 3-inch circle of sod that is planted around 1/2 ft to 1 foot apart. The idea is that these plugs will expand out and fill in the lawn completely when given enough time to do so.

Plugging is less expensive than laying down sod, as there is less material to purchase. Again, like other methods for planting your lawn, make sure your soil is optimized for vegetative growth before laying down plugs.

Now, dig a relatively shallow hole of about 3 inches deep, place the plugs equidistant throughout the property, and roll the plugs down with a weighted roller after they are in place. Then, water the plugs at least once a day for a few weeks to encourage root formation and expansion.

STRIP SODDING

Strip sodding is another technique for planting your lawn that falls in between sodding your lawn and plugging. Simply put, the idea with strip sodding is to lay rows of sod with about 8 inches between each row. So instead of laying sod directly next to the row before it, leave a spacer and allow the lawn to grow in with time. After placing the strip sod in place, roll it down, and water it as you would with sod.

CHAPTER 4 - RENOVATING YOUR LAWN

In this chapter, I'm going to assume that you already have an established lawn, but you aren't satisfied with it and want to completely renovate it and start anew. Most people are in this situation, as they are just fed up with how their lawn looks and realize that it needs a complete overhaul if it is ever to achieve near perfection.

How To Decide Whether Or Not To Renovate Your Lawn

It may be a difficult choice to decide whether you should nurse your lawn back to health or start over again and renovate your lawn from scratch.

The general guidelines on whether or not you should renovate your lawn include what percentage of your current lawn is healthy. If less than 50% of your lawn contains healthy grass, it is best to start over from scratch and renovate it completely.

If the grass variety isn't appropriate for your climate or you would rather have another species of grass, it is best to start over and renovate your lawn.

If your current lawn is loaded with weeds and it would be easier to kill all the weeds and the grass, renovating your lawn is the best choice.

If your wife or husband complains about your lawn, renovating your lawn from scratch is definitely the best choice.

Let's take a look at both renovating a cold-climate lawn and a warm-climate lawn, as there are some slight differences.

RENOVATING YOUR COLD-CLIMATE LAWN

Performing A Full Lawn Renovation

A full lawn renovation requires us to kill the old lawn and weeds so we can start over from scratch or in this case, dirt. The best time to initialize a lawn renovation project is in the summer when you will completely kill off the lawn before renovating the lawn with seed or sod in the fall time.

Measuring Out The Lawn

With any seeding project, we need to know exactly how much seed we have to buy so it is mandatory to measure out the lawn and determine the square footage.

Buying The Perfect Grass Seed

Now, purchase the grass seed that you plan to plant before even starting this project so you ensure that you have it on hand and are ready to go when it is needed. Again, as stated before, purchase the best seeds you can get, one that is genetically optimized for your environmental conditions.

Install The Irrigation System

Installing an irrigation system is completely optional, but if you are going to do it, now is the time to break open the soil and add it before the renovation. If you don't plan to use an irrigation system, at least have a sprinkler system ready to go when it comes time to water the seeds so they are constantly moist.

Kill Off The Grass And Weeds

While no one wants a completely dead lawn in the middle of summer, you are going to have to accept that your lawn is going to look awful and be a literal scar on the entire neighborhood during this time. Like a Phoenix rising out of the ashes, we need to start with soil before we can rebuild.

Using RoundUp To Kill Off The Lawn

The most common way to kill off your lawn is to apply glyphosate, sold under the brand name Roundup. Make one application of a 41% concentration of Roundup during the summer, typically mid-July, and wait two weeks before applying another application of Roundup of the same strength. This will ensure that all the weeds, even ones that are just sprouting, are killed off before the seeding project.

After applying the first application of Roundup, water your lawn regularly even though you can see it dying before your eyes. While this may seem illogical, the reason why we water the lawn now is so weeds and grass that weren't killed off by the first application of Roundup can grow, enabling them to be killed off by the second application of Roundup.

Using A Rototiller To Kill Off Your Lawn

If you don't want to use chemicals to kill off your lawn, you can also use a rototiller to bring you back to a blank slate of bare dirt. First, rototill your lawn completely and then water your lawn for around 10 days. This will give weeds a chance to regrow before rototilling again. After this, water your lawn for another 10 days and rototill it a third time.

Rototilling your way to bare soil requires far more effort than using Roundup, but it is a chemical-free option.

Using A Plastic Tarp To Kill Off Your Lawn

Another option is to use a black plastic tarp to cover your entire lawn so all plants die off due to a lack of sunlight. After dropping the plastic in place, cover it with heavy objects like stones to hold it there. Typically, lay down this plastic in the early summer so all plants are dead by the time it is time to renovate your lawn in the early fall.

Timing A Lawn Renovation

Plan all this accordingly and make sure that you have enough time between applying Roundup, using the rototiller, or laying down a plastic sheet in the summer and renovating your lawn in the fall time, typically in mid-September.

Scalping The Lawn

By the time fall comes around, your lawn should be completely dead so it is time to prepare it for the seeding project. First, mow the lawn as low as possible to remove the buildup of dead plant material.

Dethatch The Lawn

Dethatching is the process of removing dead plant matter from your lawn. While you can manually perform this operation with a dethatching rake, it is a significant workout that you might not want to undertake. Dethatching the lawn with a rake requires vigorous raking to remove all of the dead plant material and expose the soil below so it can then be removed by a lawn mower with a bag attachment. The goal of this dethatching process is to expose more soil area so the grass seeds have the best shot of germination.

Instead of manually dethatching, many people either purchase or rent a dethatching machine. This is my recommendation so you can quickly perform the dethatching process and get on with the project.

Core Aeration

Now, perform core aeration to further expose the soil area to the soon-to-be planted grass seed. Performing core aeration increases germination potential and further pushes us closer to seeding day.

Leveling And Rolling The Soil

To level the soil, add in screened topsoil and use a leveling rake or a four-wheeler with a leveling attachment to completely smooth out the soil so the new lawn doesn't have any bumps or grooves that are both unsightly and make maintenance more difficult.

A mistake I often see beginners make is using sand during this initial leveling process, but topsoil is far better, as it enhances seed germination. Only use sand as a way to level your yard after the lawn is already established.

After leveling the soil, roll the soil and compact it down to ensure that there are no bumps or grooves. If so, add a bit more topsoil, level it out again, and roll the soil down again.

Seed The Lawn

Finally, the big day has come, it is time to seed the lawn. Take a look at the bags of seeds that you bought and glance at the seeding rate on the side of the bag so you know exactly how much to apply to a particular square foot area.

After weighing out the proper amount of seeds for a particular area, use a spreader to apply those seeds in a random pattern, ensuring that they are all evenly distributed over the lawn.

If you want a lawn that fills in quickly, consider planting Tall Fescue, or Perennial Ryegrass, as it grows considerably faster than Kentucky Bluegrass seeds. However, if you have time and are patient, and enjoy the look of Kentucky Bluegrass, just realize it will take more time to fill in.

Apply Fertilizer

Applying starter fertilizer will ensure quick growth after the seeds have germinated and are forming roots. Typically granular fertilizer is best for this application, as it is released slowly over the next couple of weeks.

Rake And Roll In The Seeds

As with any seeding project, after the seeds are in the soil, rake them into the ground to improve soil contact. After raking in the seeds, roll in the seeds to compact the soil down so it improves germination rates.

Cover The Seeds With Peat Moss

Covering the seeds with a layer of peat moss ensures that the soil will retain a high moisture content and offer some protection from predators. Ideally, use a peat moss rolling spreader that can be rented in your area.

Add A Top Dressing
Like Straw Or Hydromulch

Now, add a top dressing over the soil to maintain moisture and protect the seeds from birds and other pests. The common top dressing is straw, but some people choose to use hydromulch or a wood fiber blanket.

Watering The Seeds

Now it comes time to water the seeds to ensure that they germinate. Initially, apply a significant amount of water so the entire soil is saturated. Going forward, the goal with watering the seeds should be to keep them moist at all times, yet not drenched in water so there shouldn't be puddles forming on your property.

If you decided to put in an irrigation system that should have been done before beginning the process of a lawn renovation. If you are using a sprinkler system to water the seeds, make sure that it is active two or three times a day and covers the entire property.

Ideally, water the lawn in the morning, mid-morning, and afternoon on a daily basis. As stated before, some grasses like Perennial Ryegrass germinate within 3 or 4 days, while Kentucky Bluegrass takes about 10 days to begin germinating. During this time, avoid any foot traffic over the lawn and just allow it to grow on its own.

Mowing The Lawn

After the grass is around 4 inches tall, usually between 2 or 3 weeks after germination, it is time to mow the lawn. Ideally, take about an inch off the grass so it doesn't cause too much stress. Before mowing, sharpen the blades to reduce overall stress on the newly developing lawn. During the first mowing, be as gentle as possible, and ideally use a manual reel lawnmower so you can pick it up and move it without turning corners and damaging new seedlings.

Fertilizing The Lawn

Around a month after seeds begin to germinate the lawn should fill in nicely and now it is time to fertilize it again. Either starter fertilizer or regular fertilizer like 10-10-10 can be applied at this time.

Fill In Bare Patches

There are logically going to be bare patches, where seeds were washed out, removed, or simply didn't germinate properly. During the entire process, check for these bare spots and quickly apply seeds at the exact same seeding rate that they were applied on the rest of the lawn. Applying seeds quickly will ensure that they grow in and look uniform with the rest of the lawn.

At this point, your lawn should be ready to go and will continue to look better as you perform the proper maintenance season after season. We will discuss seasonal maintenance in the next chapter.

Maintaining The Lawn After A Renovation

After the lawn has grown in nicely, it is time to start cutting it a bit lower, generally around 2 inches to 2 1/2 in, depending on the grass type. Ideally, mow the grass every time the lawn grows an inch higher than this cut height so the grass becomes accustomed to this routine.

At this point, you won't need to water the lawn 2 or 3 times a day and can let the ground dry out some and only irrigate when necessary. However, when you do irrigate, add more water than you initially did, something like a 15-minute period instead of a 5-minute period since you will be watering less frequently.

At some point, you are going to want to perform a soil test so you can customize the fertilizer for exactly what your lawn needs and avoid adding nutrients that are over-represented. We will talk more about customizing fertilizer later. In the meantime, apply a fertilizer like 10-10-10.

Now that the lawn has been renovated and has grown nicely, winter is quickly approaching. When spring comes around again, it will be time to pick up the maintenance and maximize the lawn during the next season so it looks like it was always there and never renovated.

Renovating Your Warm-Climate Lawn

If you haven't read through renovating your cold-climate lawn, do so, as nearly all of the information is the same. The only difference is that renovating a warm-climate lawn is best done in the springtime before the hot summer months encourage the newly renovated grass to grow quickly.

CHAPTER 5 - CARING FOR YOUR LAWN BY SEASON

HOW TO CARE FOR COLD-CLIMATE LAWNS SEASON BY SEASON

Spring Season

A new year is upon us, the birds are chirping, the weather is warming up, and spring is here. This is my favorite time of year, not only because I hate the cold of winter, but because it's time to get my lawn in order and spend time outside, enjoying the smell of freshly cut grass.

If your lawn is already established and doesn't require an overseeding coming out of winter, it might be a good idea to add pre-emergent herbicide now. However, a pre-emergent is not always necessary every single year if you have already removed weeds from your lawn. Personally, I don't apply pre-emergent herbicide anymore, as I don't need it.

Applying Pre-Emergent Herbicide

If you have an issue with weeds, especially crabgrass, and want to add pre-emergent herbicide, the best time to do that is when the soil temperature rises to around 50°F. It is crucial to get pre-emergent on the ground before the soil temperature rises above 55°F, as weeds will quickly begin to grow when temperatures soar higher than this. Simply go outside and stick a thermometer about 2 inches into the soil and apply pre-emergent if the temperature is over 50°F, yet under 55°F.

Dethatching And Core Aerating In The Spring Time

After the winter, there will be debris throughout your lawn so either take a dethatching rake and remove this matter or take a dethatching machine and clean up your lawn.

Next, core aerating the soil while it is still damp, but not soaking wet, is a good idea. This process increases the amount of airflow, and water access, while making it easier for fertilizer to reach the roots of your grass.

Keep A Look Out For Common Spring Diseases

When looking over your lawn after winter, look for evidence of Snow Mold, Fairy Rings, Ring Spot, and Red Thread. If you can pinpoint these diseases quickly, they are easier to treat than if you let them expand.

Pest Control In The Spring

There are certain pests specific to spring that you will have to look out for and eradicate if they are damaging your lawn. As earthworms venture up into the top layers of soil, moles take this opportunity to feast on them. Moles destroy a lawn's root system by tunneling through it when searching for food.

The best way to deal with moles is to set up animal traps immediately in the spring. If you don't get a handle on the infestation of moles, they will be there all year digging tunnels throughout your yard.

Overseeding In The Spring Time

If you are looking to fill in some bare spots or damaged grass that was still left over from fall, you can overseed your lawn now, but realize that you can't also use a pre-emergent at the same time. The steps of overseeding your lawn were explained in the previous chapter so I won't go over them again.

Should I Apply Fertilizer Immediately In The Spring?

Typically, the answer is no, you don't need to apply fertilizer in the early springtime, as it already has enough fertilizer left over from last year. If you didn't apply fertilizer consistently last year and are just starting to improve your lawn now, this is a good time to apply fertilizer to get this process in motion.

74

Mowing Your Lawn

As the snow begins to melt and the rain begins, most grass is matted down so wait a while for it to come back to life again before doing much. As soon as your lawn starts growing, it is time to start mowing it and consistently doing so throughout the season. Properly mowing your lawn is the number one way, outside of grass genetics, water, and fertilizer, to make your lawn look as excellent as possible.

Get in the habit of mowing your lawn at least twice a week, but ideally, once every 3 days. While that may seem like craziness to most people who don't understand what lawn maintenance entails, a consistent mowing schedule will keep the lawn at the ideal height and reduce weed formation. At the very least, aim to mow your lawn at least once a week, but in my honest opinion, this is not frequent enough for it to look its absolute best.

Depending on your lawn type and how short you want to mow it, set up your mower at that specific height and maintain it throughout the season, assuming you are cutting your lawn at regular intervals.

If you didn't maintain your lawnmower before you stored it away for winter, now is the time to change the oil, sharpen the blades, and clean out the deck. Realize that you should be sharpening the blades often to ensure a clean cut that reduces the amount of stress on the grass.

If you have Tall Fescue grass, aim to cut a bit more than an inch off your lawn when it grows to about 4 inches, dropping it down to just below 3 inches. As the name applies, Tall Fescue enjoys a higher cut than the other grasses and looks best at about 3 inches.

If you have Kentucky Bluegrass, you can cut it quite short, as low as 1/2 inch with a reel mower, but most people cut it at right around 2 inches. When Kentucky Bluegrass grows to about 3 inches high, cut it down 1 inch to the ideal 2-inch cut height.

Perennial Ryegrass is another option that can be cut quite short. Again, Perennial Ryegrass can be cut as short as Kentucky Bluegrass and even shorter if it is cut properly. The best way to cut these grass types as short as possible is to use a reel mower and slowly drop down to the cut height you prefer so you don't overstress the grass initially.

Applying Post-Emergent

As the grass revives itself during the spring, there may be some weeds that sprouted through even if you applied a pre-emergent. At this time, it is best to apply post-emergent herbicide. If weeds aren't everywhere throughout your lawn, you can apply a product like Weed B-gon to spots that have undesirable weeds like dandelion, chickweed, dollarweed, and clover.

Watering Your Lawn In Spring

Depending on where you are located, if your spring season is relatively dry you will want to consider watering your lawn on a regular basis so it looks its best. However, in most locations where spring is rainy, Mother Nature should provide all the irrigation you need during this time of the year. In any case, be prepared to water your lawn if it isn't raining enough, aiming for at least 1 inch of water on your lawn per week.

Taking A Soil Sample

If you didn't take a soil sample during the last season, the best way to know exactly what your grass needs is to take a soil sample now.

Applying Fertilizer In Late Spring

Late spring is the time for the first application of fertilizer, assuming you didn't apply it immediately in early spring. With the results of your soil analysis, you can customize your fertilizer. You can choose granular fertilizer or spray fertilizer, assuming you have the equipment to do so. If you don't have a soil analysis, a 10-10-10 fertilizer is the go-to option.

Another thing to look at is the micronutrients, as they certainly contribute to the health of your lawn. Specifically, iron is important in keeping your lawn green throughout the hot days of summer when all other lawns in your neighborhood have turned brown.

Summer Season

As we enter the summer months, caring for your lawn requires less effort than in spring since the grass grows slower in hot weather. Make sure your lawn has enough water and modify the number of times you mow your lawn based on the growth rate.

In midsummer, most cold-weather grasses end up turning brown, as they go dormant during this extremely hot period. While not detrimental to the grass over the long term, as it comes back strong in the fall, it is unsightly and

77

there are ways to help prevent cold weather grasses from going dormant in the hot summer.

Watering And Fertilizing
Your Lawn In The Summer

In addition to regular watering, applying a diluted fertilizer solution that includes iron and other micronutrients is one way to help keep your lawn green throughout the summer. Typically, apply this weak fertilizer solution once every 2 to 3 weeks. Upon seeing your grass, your neighbors will definitely ask how you are keeping your lawn green when they are unable to even though they are watering it more than you are. Be aware that it is not necessary to fertilize your lawn in the summer, but anyone after an ideal curb appeal will benefit by adding small amounts of fertilizer.

You won't have to put a huge amount of water on your lawn during the summer if you are located in a humid area. From an external perspective, it seems like you are using a water tower's worth of water to keep your lawn so green. However, irrigating your lawn with about an inch of water a week is enough to maintain it during the summer months. Apply water during the morning hours or the afternoon hours so it doesn't immediately evaporate when the sun hits it. Keep an eye on your grass and notice when the edges of the lawn start wilting slightly. This is the best day to add water, as your lawn is just beginning to dehydrate.

If your soil always seems dry no matter how much you water your lawn, there are certain wetting agents that make the soil less hydrophobic and hold onto water better. This allows the soil to remain moist throughout the summer when it would typically be dry.

There are certain cultivars that are perfect for various regions and with advances in science, there are many new grass types that are easier to keep green during the hot summer months. As stated before, if you have a chance to start your lawn from scratch, take your time and do your research to find the absolute best grass seeds for you.

Mowing Your Lawn In Summer

Keep mowing your lawn when it needs to be cut based on how fast it is growing. Many people allow their lawns to grow higher and increase the cut height to avoid over-stressing it during the summer. Summer is a good time to sharpen the blades on your lawnmower so it cuts the grass cleanly, reducing stress.

Keep A Look Out For
Common Summer Diseases

When looking over your lawn in summer, look for evidence of Necrotic Ring Spot, Fairy Rings, Red Thread, Dollar Spot, Rust, Summer Patch, and Powdery Mildew. Typically, these diseases are the result of watering your lawn before nightfall. To avoid these fungal diseases, water your lawn in the morning or afternoon instead of before dusk.

Pest Control In The Summer

There are certain pests specific to summer that can damage your lawn if you are complacent. Summer pests include turf caterpillars, grubs, and sod webworms, among other insects. Sod webworms are especially worrisome, as they can literally eat your entire lawn within days!

The best way to deal with these pests is to inspect your lawn on a daily basis and kill off these pests as soon as you notice them.

Post-Emergent Summer Application

If weeds are an issue in the summer, you can apply post-emergent herbicide at this time. Ideally, search for an herbicide with quinclorac or fenoxaprop. When applying herbicides during the summer, only do so when the temperature is below 85°F to avoid overstressing your lawn. If weeds aren't overly populated, just pick out weeds by hand.

Fall Season

As we approach the end of summer, temperatures drop consistently and cold-weather lawns start turning green again and growing quickly. Even if you allowed your lawn to go dormant over the summer, it should come bouncing back in the fall in splendid fashion.

Fertilizing In The Fall

When temperatures have dropped back into the 70s, it is typically the time to add more fertilizer, irrigate if necessary, and keep up with your mowing so the grass doesn't grow out of control.

Select fertilizer that offers slow-release nitrogen so it is continuously released throughout the rest of the year and the grass maintains a green vibrance. Additionally, choose a fertilizer with a high quantity of potassium that will assist the growth of roots if you plan on overseeding. Typically, phosphorus needs will be covered by this time so you can choose a fertilizer like 24-0-10. This will give you high quantities of nitrogen, no phosphorus at all, and medium quantities of potassium. Again, having a soil sample will allow you to customize your fertilizer needs.

The best time to fertilize your lawn is after a decent rainfall or irrigation. Never apply fertilizer when the lawn is dry.

Fall Lawn Renovations

The fall season is the time to perform any renovations, either small, spot renovations or full-scale renovations, assuming you already took the preparatory steps to do so.

In most cases, there will be some damage that will need to be fixed, like dog spots, bare spots, and dead areas. This work should be completed now, so it can grow before winter strikes. Additionally, there will likely be debris that has built up and should be removed so the lawn doesn't contain dead material preventing the grass from filling in these spots.

Removing Debris From
Your Lawn In Early Fall

To properly remove excess debris from your lawn, cut it a little bit lower than normal, typically as low as 2 inches so the thatch can easily be removed. I regress, as 'easy' might not be the correct word choice if you are using a dethatching rake. If you have access to a dethatching machine, run that over the entire lawn and remove the built-up debris. Then, go back over the lawn looking for spots that weren't completely cleaned and use the dethatching rake to completely remove unsightly debris. Finally, run your lawnmower over the debris and collect all the thatch in the bag so you don't have to rake it all up and pick it up by hand.

At the end of this project, you should be able to see down to the soil in most areas, allowing the existing sod to expand and fill up those places.

Core Aeration In Fall

Performing core aeration in the fall is the best time to do so, especially if your lawn received a lot of foot traffic over the summer. When core aerating, focus special attention on areas that were trampled down. Aerating your soil will allow water and nutrients to enter the soil easily, and remedy overly compacted soil. After dethatching and core aeration, water the lawn and fertilize if you don't plan on overseeding.

Overseeding In The Fall

Overseeding in the fall is the perfect time of year to fill in bare spots and get the lawn in perfect shape before winter. Ideally, follow the rates for overseeding your lawn that are listed on the side of the bag so you drop adequate grass seeds on your lawn. Overseeding should be performed after dethatching and core aeration so these seeds will have more contact with the soil below the turf. After overseeding your lawn, apply fertilizer and water so the seeds germinate and quickly fill in the turf.

Mowing Your Lawn In The Fall

Keep up with your mowing during the fall and continue to maintain the same cut height that you were during the spring season. As we move closer to the end of the year, the grass will grow slower so you won't need to cut quite as often.

Many people stop cutting their lawns in the late fall, but allowing the grass to grow too long may allow fungal diseases to develop quickly. Continue to keep up your mowing until the grass is clearly not growing anymore, generally when daytime high temperatures are in the 40s and night temperatures are dropping into the 20s.

Watering Your Lawn In The Fall

While temperatures are cooler than in the summer, your lawn still needs adequate water during the fall months. Ideally, keep an eye on your lawn and look for small patches near the edges that are wilting up and immediately irrigate the grass to avoid dehydration. As a general rule, maintain at least 1 inch of water on your lawn per week until at least the end of October.

Common Fall Lawn Diseases

During the fall, your lawn is susceptible to a number of different diseases including Fairy Rings, Necrotic Ring Spot, Rust, and Red Thread. Check your lawn on a regular basis, ideally every single day, and handle any of these diseases quickly if they appear.

Small Renovation Projects In The Fall

For small, little renovation projects, simply remove as much of the dead material from the area as possible so there is plenty of soil exposure. Then, apply grass seed to the area, and follow all the steps in regard to seeding your lawn that were discussed earlier. Grass should quickly grow back in these locations and look decent in time for winter.

Winter Season

When preparing for winter, move any excess lawn seeds and liquids you are storing in your storage shed to a location where they won't freeze, potentially in your basement. Everything that is going to be left in the shed over winter should be winterized including the lawnmower.

Winterizing The Lawnmower

Either remove all the gasoline from the lawnmower and run it until it is out of gas or add a fuel stabilizer to the gasoline so it lasts until next spring. Change the oil in the lawnmower and sharpen the blades so it is ready for another season of action. Now, wash your lawn mower and dry it. If there are any rusty spots, touch up those areas.

Remove the spark plug and add a little bit of motor oil to the cylinder. Something like a tablespoon is enough. Then, lubricate all the moving parts including the choke and throttle.

Check all the belts and replace any that are worn out. If you have a riding lawnmower, remove the battery and store it in the basement.

HOW TO CARE FOR WARM-CLIMATE LAWNS SEASON BY SEASON

Many aspects of caring for a warm-climate lawn are similar to a cold-climate lawn, but there are some small differences, especially in regard to timing.

Spring Season

In early spring, right around March, begin to start mowing your lawn once you notice that it is growing. At this point, it is a good time for a soil test so you can accurately add amendments back into the soil to obtain the proper pH, mineral levels, and other nutrients.

Dethatching And Core Aeration

Spring is the ideal time to dethatch and perform core aeration. Both improve soil drainage, reduce soil compaction, and reduce the probability of disease. The idea is to remove dead plant matter to improve the overseeding germination rate and to help the grass expand over the summer.

Overseeding Your Lawn In Spring

Spring is the time for overseeding your lawn before the summertime. Typically, wait for soil temperatures to reach right around 65°F before spreading seed throughout your lawn. The process of overseeding is exactly like a cold-climate lawn so follow the steps that were highlighted earlier in this chapter.

85

Watering Your Lawn

In the springtime, most areas of the warm-climate portion of the nation should receive sufficient precipitation. If required, supplement rain with irrigation so your lawn receives at least 1 inch of water a week.

Summer Season

As summer sets in, your grass will begin growing rapidly so apply fertilizer every month or every 2 months at the minimum. Additionally, continue watering your grass to ensure it is receiving at least 1 inch of water per week. Typically, most places require more irrigation at the end of the summer season, as rainfall may be limited.

Mowing Your Lawn In The Summer

Adjust the height of your lawnmower to allow your grass to grow higher during the summertime. The reasons for this are that longer grass is able to maintain soil moisture and choke out weeds. Cut your lawn regularly throughout the summer months and only take off 1/3 to bring it down to the ideal cut height.

Checking The Lawn For Pests
Like Grub Worms

If there are pests like grub worms, take active steps against them so they don't become a problem. More information on pests is in Chapter 7.

Fall Season

As we enter the fall, now is a good time to apply a pre-emergent herbicide, generally when temperatures have subsided to somewhere between 65°F and 70°F at night. This will prevent weeds from growing as we move into the cooler season and reduce the amount of post-emergent herbicide we will have to use heading into spring.

Overseeding Your Lawn With Cold Climate Grasses

If you don't apply a pre-emergent herbicide, you can overseed your lawn at this time with cold-climate grasses that will maintain a lush, green color over winter. Typically, Perennial Ryegrass is the cold-climate grass of choice, as it grows quickly and should become fully established before winter kicks in.

The process for overseeding warm-climate grasses is the same as cold-climate grasses described earlier in the chapter.

Mowing Your Lawn In The Fall

Continue to mow your lawn throughout the fall until you notice that your grass is not growing anymore. If you overseed your lawn with cold-climate grass, you will need to continue to mow throughout the winter, as this grass thrives in cooler conditions.

Winter Season

Assuming that you overseeded your lawn with cold-climate grasses, continue to fertilize, water, and mow your lawn on a normal schedule that is consistent with cold-climate grasses.

If weeds have developed, spot-treat them with a post-emergent herbicide.

Lawn Care Consistency

Following a regular schedule to care for your lawn year after year will go a long way in making it look its best. Like anything else in life, success is directly related to consistency so stay on schedule and enjoy watching your lawn improve year after year.

CHAPTER 6 -
WATERING, FERTILIZING
AND MOWING

The biggest factors that will have the greatest effect on your lawn are watering it, fertilizing it, and mowing it. Here we will take a detailed look at each aspect of perfecting your lawn.

ALL ABOUT WATERING
YOUR LAWN

After your lawn is established, it should only be watered when it begins to dry out, meaning you don't have to stick to a regular schedule of watering like you would when your lawn is first developing.

Many homeowners get into the habit of watering their lawns on a weekly basis, but in most cases, this simply isn't necessary. While it might not seem like a bad thing to over-water your lawn, it actually contributes to a higher potential for disease, especially fungus, more weeds, and of course, even more mowing.

When deciding when to water your lawn, consider the weather forecast, the temperature, the overall humidity, how windy it is, and whether or not it rained recently or will rain soon.

After you have an established lawn, focus on watering thoroughly so all the water soaks into the soil below. If you do this, you won't need to water your lawn very often, as it should maintain moisture for a while. The general rule is to soak the soil all the way down to 7 inches below the surface. To check this, stick a screwdriver or some other tool into the soil and note whether it is wet at the depth you are looking for.

Watering Different Soil Types

The type of soil you have will determine how well the water is able to absorb into the soil. In soil that contains sand, watering should take place in 1-inch intervals so the water doesn't all wash away without being absorbed. In this case, use the sprinkler until water has entered the depth of 1 inch and move it to another location while coming back time and time again to ensure that water has eventually absorbed into the soil 7 inches deep. This will ensure water saturation without simply being flushed away. If your soil has high quantities of sand in it, you will need to irrigate it more often, sometimes as much as 3 times a week.

In soil that contains a high content of clay, the water will quickly run off without being absorbed. When you notice water starting to run off, cycle the sprinkler to another location and then back to the original location until absorption reaches down to the depth you are looking for. If your soil consists of high quantities of clay, it will hold onto water better and won't need to be irrigated as frequently.

After running these sprinkler systems and reaching the desired moisture saturation soil depth, make a note of the amount of time it took and water your lawn for the same duration each time, assuming similar weather conditions. If the weather is hotter or windier than normal water a bit longer.

The Benefits Of Watering Thoroughly

A thorough watering encourages deep root growth and improves the overall health of your lawn. On the contrary, if you only water lightly and do so frequently, the roots won't have any reason to grow deeper, as they have all the water they need on the surface. Another disadvantage of watering frequently, yet lightly is that the soil will constantly remain drenched, reducing soil oxygen absorption that in time can choke out the roots below and kill them.

A thorough watering will maintain deep soil moisture even when the surface dries up. As the roots grow deeper, they are able to survive better during the midsummer heat wave and your lawn will remain green far longer than your neighbors.

Irrigation System

An inground irrigation system or mobile sprinkler system is recommended so you don't completely depend on mother nature to water your lawn. As far as sprinkler systems, options include the impact sprinkler, oscillating sprinkler, and traveling sprinkler. My personal favorite is

91

the traveling sprinkler, the one designed like a small tractor that my grandparents had, as it always fascinated me. The traveling sprinkler allows you to sprinkle water on the largest area with the least amount of work, as the makeshift tractor runs from one side of your lawn to the other.

When choosing a sprinkler system, take a look at the fine print and note how many square feet they are able to cover. Since you should already know the square footage of your lawn, this information will allow you to hone in on the sprinkler system setup that is able to cover your entire lawn.

If you don't install an in-ground sprinkler system that covers your entire yard, choose a combination of mobile sprinklers that include oscillating sprinklers and revolving sprinklers to cover most of the yard, and impact sprinklers to cover small, irregularly shaped areas.

When choosing a sprinkler or irrigation system, spend the money on a quality product, as cheap knockoffs often break quickly, forcing you to replace them, and in the end, costing more money overall.

As a general rule, apply somewhere between 1 inch and 2 inches of water weekly to your grass. Realize that this also includes rainfall so calculate this in. To determine how much rain has fallen, place a measuring cup or glass somewhere on your property and take note of the water level after rain. Then, adjust your irrigation amount accordingly.

When Is The Best Time To Water My Lawn?

Morning is unequivocally the best time to water your lawn. The reason for this is that the sun won't be as high in the sky, causing excessive evaporation so the water will be able to remain in the soil for a longer period of time.

Additionally, this will allow more water to seep into the soil and make contact with the roots.

Watering your lawn before night or in the nighttime significantly increases the potential for disease, as fungus will quickly develop if the grass is left wet all night long. If you are going to water later in the day, do so in the afternoon, so your lawn will be just about dry by nighttime.

Avoid watering your lawn during midday, as most of that water will quickly evaporate and never reach the grass root system.

Grass located near trees and other vegetation will need to be watered more often, as it is competing with these other plants for moisture. Keep a close eye on areas like this and give them water on a regular basis so they don't end up drying up.

Should I Use A Wetting Agent?

If you are having an issue with your lawn drying out quickly, you may want to use a wetting agent to optimize the water you sprinkle onto your lawn. These wetting compounds are able to hold onto water for a longer period of time, maintaining soil moisture.

There are many of these products on the market that will enable your lawn to be more resistant to droughts and diseases while using less water overall. Typically, most homeowners won't require a wetting agent to keep their lawn hydrated if they follow the correct watering procedures.

How Do I Know When To Water My Lawn?

Ideally, water your lawn before it needs water, far before it dries out noticeably. When your lawn needs water, it will change in color, look less luscious, and the blades of grass will noticeably curl up lengthwise. The grass does this to conserve water as much as possible.

You will know when your grass needs water if you walk on it and it doesn't immediately return to its original form. Instead, your footprints will remain visible long after you stepped on the grass.

If your lawn starts turning brown, then it is clearly calling out for water. If you don't take steps now to rehydrate it, it may never recover fully.

If you are correctly irrigating your lawn, as described above, it should never get to this point.

ALL ABOUT FERTILIZING
YOUR LAWN

Fertilizer comes in three different forms, ones that provide the macronutrients, nitrogen, phosphorus, and potassium, secondary nutrients, and micronutrients. Let's take a look at each of these aspects starting with the macronutrients first.

Macronutrients - Nitrogen

As stated by the name, macronutrients are the most important fertilizer you will be applying to your lawn. Nitrogen allows your grass to grow quickly and maintains

94

its green color. A lack of nitrogen results in grass that turns yellow and withers away. It is important to keep a consistent supply of nitrogen on your lawn, as it leaches out of the soil quickly. Realize that while nitrogen is extremely important, putting too much nitrogen on your lawn can burn your grass.

Nitrogen-based fertilizers come in either fast-release or slow-release options, and typically, a combination of both.

Fast-Release Nitrogen Fertilizer

Fast-release nitrogen formulas include ammonium sulfate, urea, and ammonium phosphate. These nitrogen-based formulas are the least expensive options available. As soon as these fast-release nitrogen fertilizers are applied to your lawn, you will notice your grass grow quickly nearly immediately. Avoid applying high quantities of these fast-release nitrogen formulas on your lawn, as they are typically the ones responsible for burning your grass, due to their high saline content. As the name applies, fast-releasing nitrogen formulas are like a short burst of energy.

Slow Release Nitrogen Fertilizer

Slow-release nitrogen fertilizers include organic animal manure, sewer sludge, and synthetic urea analogs, like IBDU and SCU.

Natural, slow-release nitrogen fertilizers like manure release nitrogen into the soil slowly, as microbes are responsible for breaking down the nitrogen and making it bioavailable. Synthetic slow-release nitrogen fertilizers have been coated by sulfur compounds and other elements so nitrogen is held onto and is released at set rates.

The benefits of slow-release nitrogen fertilizers are obvious, as they don't have to be applied constantly since they slowly break down over time, feeding your lawn at regular intervals. Of course, these slow-release nitrogen fertilizers are more expensive than their fast-release counterparts.

A Combination Of Slow And Fast Release Nitrogen Fertilizer

For the best bang for your buck, choose a fertilizer that has both fast-release and slow-release nitrogen fertilizer in it so it immediately gives your grass a boost and continues to feed it over time as well.

Macronutrients - Phosphorus

Phosphorus is the next macronutrient that is required for shoot growth and root formation. Generally, most soils around the country already have enough phosphorus so make sure this is the case with your soil test and you may not have to add as much phosphorus as is typically recommended.

The phosphorus that is available in fertilizer, P205, requires time before it is able to reach the root system, as it isn't water-soluble like nitrogen. In other words, if you have a phosphorus deficiency, it will take some time to correct in an established lawn.

Again, your soil analysis will determine how much phosphorus you need to add to your soil and if it is low, ideally add this phosphorus in before planting your lawn so it is ready to initiate root development.

I had an issue with an excess of phosphorus in my soil a few years back and if I continued to apply typical fertilizer that contains copious amounts of phosphorus, the imbalance would have become even worse. With the results of my soil test, I scaled back on the phosphorus application and focused more on increasing the nitrogen and potassium ratio. This made a huge difference in the overall appearance of my lawn, as it quickly took on a dark green hue.

Macronutrients - Potassium

Potassium is the last macronutrient that improves the health of your lawn, as it assists in keeping weeds at bay and helps your lawn during stressful conditions. A lawn that has enough potassium has a higher resistance to heat, cold, and drought-like conditions. Additionally, potassium improves wear resistance so it is especially important in lawns that receive a lot of foot traffic.

In typical fertilizers, potash, otherwise known as K20, is the form of potassium applied to your lawn. Ideally, use higher quantities of potassium if your soil is on the sandy side, as it has a tendency to leach out.

If your lawn suffers from potassium deficiency, it doesn't display a lot of obvious symptoms so the best way to determine whether or not you need to add more potassium is to get a soil test.

Secondary Nutrients

Secondary nutrients are already typically common in most soils so they don't generally need to be added in. However, the results of your soil test should indicate how much calcium, sulfur, and magnesium your soil has. In cases where the pH of your soil is out of the neutral range, calcium and magnesium increase pH, while sulfur reduces it.

Micronutrients

Micronutrients should also already be contained in your soil. As the name suggests, there don't need to be many of these minerals for adequate grass formation. The micronutrients that grass needs to grow include iron, manganese, copper, zinc, boron, chlorine, and molybdenum.

The levels of all these micronutrients should be available on any good soil test and it is easy to add them back into the soil if there is a deficiency. Typically, only an iron deficiency displays obvious side effects, as grass grown in iron-deficient soil is often yellow. However, most full-spectrum fertilizers contain iron so you shouldn't run into this deficiency often.

Applying Fertilizer

I know I harp on this over and over but the first step before applying fertilizer is to get a soil test. After your lawn is established, it is a good idea to test your soil at least every 3 years, as conditions may have changed.

What If I Don't Want To Get A Soil Test?

To each their own, and if you don't want to get your soil tested, there are some basic guidelines to follow when fertilizing your lawn. First of all, choose a fertilizer with an equivalent amount of nitrogen that is recommended for the grass species you have.

Typically, grass species require between 1 lb and 6 lbs of nitrogen per every 1000 square feet per year. For cold-climate grasses, Fescue is on the low end and Kentucky Bluegrass is on the high end of nitrogen requirements. For warm-climate grass options, Centipede grass is on the low end and Saint Augustine grass is on the high end.

Selecting The Right Fertilizer

As with anything, higher-end, quality fertilizers are going to cost more than cheap options. Of course, you get what you pay for. If you already invested significantly in your lawn and I will assume you have if you are reading this book, purchase the best fertilizers you can get if you want the best results.

Reading The Label On A Bag Of Fertilizer

The main number that stands out on a bag of fertilizer corresponds with the ratio between nitrogen, phosphorus, and potassium. For instance, if fertilizer is something like 10-10-10, it is equal parts of all three macronutrients. Then, take a look at which type of nitrogen, slow-release, fast-release, or a combination of both, is in this fertilizer formula.

If you want to know how much nitrogen specifically is in a package of fertilizer, take the number that corresponds with nitrogen and divide it by the weight of the bag. For instance, in the example above of a 10-10-10 formula that weighs 100 lbs, there is 10 lbs of nitrogen. This will allow you to use your lawn's square footage to calculate how much fertilizer you will need for your grass type over the course of an entire year.

Other information on the label of a package of fertilizer is the secondary and micronutrients that it contains.

You may be asking yourself, what is the rest of the material in a bag of fertilizer?

The majority of the weight in a bag of fertilizer is a carrier that allows the fertilizer to move deeper into the soil without releasing its nutrition immediately. This allows the fertilizer to expand its coverage.

Customized Fertilizer

With a soil analysis, you can customize your fertilizer. For instance, if you have adequate or too much phosphorus in your soil, purchase a bag of fertilizer with only nitrogen and potassium in it. Or, if you only want a nitrogen-based fertilizer, purchase that exclusively with no phosphorus or potassium in it.

Granular Fertilizer Or Liquid Fertilizer

Both granular fertilizer and liquid fertilizer are basically exactly the same. The only difference is how they are applied. Typically, fertilizer in granule form is easier to spread throughout your yard whereas liquid fertilizer requires a hose and an attachment that must be repeatedly refilled.

When To Apply Fertilizer?

Fertilize your lawn when your grass is dry. After you are done fertilizing, irrigate your lawn so the fertilizer runs down into the soil. The problem with fertilizing your lawn when it is wet is that fertilizer sticks to the grass itself and can end up burning it, especially in the presence of the sun.

What Time Of Year
Should I Fertilize My Lawn?

While there are some general rules, the best times to fertilize your lawn are based on your grass type, your climate, and a number of other factors including the weather. Ideally, fertilize your lawn before it is about to enter a period of significant growth, that takes place in the spring and fall for cold climate grasses. Warm climate grasses should be fertilized in the late spring, summer, and early fall, as they grow significantly during these times of the year.

How Many Times Of Year
Should I Fertilize My Lawn?

Again, how many times a year you fertilize your lawn will depend on your grass type and how much maintenance you want to put in. At the very least, just to keep your grass alive, you will need to fertilize it once a year. For lawn types that are relatively low maintenance, fertilizing twice a year is generally sufficient. A step up from that usually requires fertilizing three times a year. Finally, a high-maintenance lawn with a grass type that requires significant fertilizer should be fertilized once a month during the growing season.

Can I Use Organic Fertilizer?

Of course, you can use organic fertilizer and I encourage using at least some organic fertilizer in addition to synthetic fertilizer, as it promotes microorganisms in the soil, improving your soil quality. Organic fertilizers like manure, compost, and even seaweed are all viable options to give your lawn the nutrition it needs. However, realize that the amount of nitrogen in organic fertilizer is far less concentrated than in synthetic fertilizers. For this reason, a combination of both organic and synthetic fertilizers is the most logical option.

If you want to completely rely on organic fertilizer for your lawn, more power to you, but realize that you are going to have to apply a lot of material to equate to the number of macronutrients that are contained in synthetic fertilizer.

Your Lawn Clippings Are Free Fertilizer

If you don't have a pressing need to bag your lawn clippings or remove them, leave them on your lawn, as the nitrogen they contain isn't going anywhere, and will decompose back into the soil. By allowing your lawn clippings to fertilize your lawn, you can save around 25% on fertilizer costs.

Using Your Spreader
To Apply Granular Fertilizer

If you are serious about lawn care you should have your own rotary or broadcast spreader. Trying to fertilize your entire lawn with a hand crank spreader is going to be a challenge, to say the least.

The label on a bag of fertilizer will indicate the spreading rate so adjust your spreader accordingly and go around your lawn evenly applying fertilizer. The best way to ensure an even application is to fertilize up and down your lawn the entire length of the lawn while walking at the same pace throughout. After covering the whole lawn, go back and spread fertilizer in between the rows that you already completed. In this way, fertilizer should be evenly distributed throughout the lawn.

If you accidentally spill a large amount of fertilizer anywhere on your lawn, take your garden hose and flush the area down completely so it doesn't burn your grass.

MOWING YOUR LAWN

Most people don't understand the difference that consistent mowing makes for the health and appearance of their lawn. However, mowing is one of the most important activities you can do to make your lawn look stellar. Here we will go into detail on the proper way to mow your lawn.

What Exactly Happens
When You Cut Your Lawn?

When you cut your lawn, the grass root system stops growing momentarily. This limits its ability to consume nutrients and water. The advantage to cutting your lawn is that new grass plants are able to sprout up, increasing your lawn's thickness. A dense lawn keeps weeds at bay, as they don't have anywhere to grow.

What Is The Perfect Height To Cut My Lawn?

While unique to each species of grass and your personal preference, the general rule is to cut your grass 1/3 of its current height. For instance, if your grass is 3 in tall and it is time to cut it, only reduce it to 2 inches tall, taking off 1 inch. If you cut it significantly shorter than that, your grass will go into shock.

What Happens If You
Cut Your Lawn Too Short?

People who only want to mow as little as possible often wait for their grass to flop over before they mow it. Then, they drop their lawnmower deck as low as possible to cut their grass at the bare minimum and repeat the cycle. Welcome to Scalp City. When the grass is scalped, the root system becomes overly stressed, allowing weeds, diseases, and pests to overtake the grass.

What Can I Do If I Cut My Grass Too Low?

If you cut your grass too low and notice that it is looking stressed out, wait until morning and then add some trace minerals like iron, calcium, and manganese. Immediately after that, irrigate your lawn. Going forward, give your lawn more water than normal and the grass should quickly return to its former glory.

Determining The Right Height For Your Grass

When determining the right height for your grass err on the side of caution and allow it to grow a bit taller than you would like and start by taking 1/3 off it. Taller grass is more heat tolerant and maintains soil moisture better, ensuring your lawn doesn't become dehydrated quickly.

Proper Cut Height For Various Grass Species

The typical cut heights for various grass species were discussed in the first chapter, but warm-climate grasses like Bermuda grass can be cut the lowest, while Buffalo grass prefers to be cut at a higher height.

Cold-climate grasses like Kentucky Bluegrass and Perennial Ryegrass prefer a cut height between about 2 inches and 3 inches. Fescue grasses prefer a cut height between 2 1/2 inches and 3 1/2 inches.

Modifying Your Cut Height
Throughout The Year

When grass is growing its fastest, it is acceptable to cut it shorter, as it quickly bounces back during these seasons. However, when grass growth begins to slow, allow it to grow out more before cutting it. For instance, if you have a cold climate glass, allow it to grow out more during the hot summer and cut it shorter during the spring and fall.

Changing Your Cut Height
Based On Lawn Conditions

Additionally, change your cut height depending on the condition of your lawn. For instance, if you are going through a drought or have issues with pests or diseases, cut the grass higher than normal to reduce overall stress.

What Is The Best Time To Cut My Grass?

The best time to cut your lawn is right before nighttime when the grass is dry. The reason for this is that sunny conditions result in more stress on both you and your grass.

As soon as your grass has reached the height you are planning to mow it at, it is best to cut it as soon as possible so it doesn't grow even higher. However, if your lawn grows out before you get a chance to mow it, only take off 1/3 of the height. For instance, if your lawn grows out to 6 inches, only mow it down to 4 inches. Then, a couple of days later, mow it down another 1/3 of its height. Continue to repeat this process until you get back to your desired cut height.

Maintaining Your Lawnmower

One thing some homeowners forget to do is sharpen up the blades on their lawnmowers on a regular basis. The sharpest blades reduce the stress on newly cut grass, as sharp blades cut the grass cleanly instead of pulling at the plant as a dull blade would do. Ideally, sharpen your blades at least 3 times a year to maintain an ideal cut. One way to know that your lawnmower blades aren't sharp enough is if your lawn looks a little bit brown the day after you cut it.

The key to sharpening your lawnmower's blades is safety first, so start by removing the distributor cap from the spark plug so for some crazy reason, it doesn't start automatically. Then, remove the blade, place it on a workbench, use a vice or clamp to hold it in place, and either use a file or an angle grinder to sharpen the blade at the correct angle.

After the blade is sharp, balance it on a cone. If it leans to one side, take off a bit more metal on that side and balance it out. Then, put the blades back on the mower, tighten them, put the distributor cap back on the spark plug, and start up the mower. Now you should be ready to go.

Time To Cut Your Lawn

Before cutting your lawn, survey it and remove any debris that may be present. If you haven't already set your blade to the height you want, do so now. Now, begin mowing your lawn, typically at the property line, all the way around the perimeter, and then around objects like your house, trees, and shrubs. Then, make your way across your lawn, mowing in rows.

Instead of lining up your wheel with the wheel mark from the last row, overlap by 2 inches to ensure that you don't miss any blades of grass. When taking corners, take your time and ideally, lift up the front of the lawnmower so that it reduces the amount of friction on the grass. If you have hills in your yard mow them at a 45° angle for safety reasons.

Every time you mow, do so in the opposite direction, a 90° angle, from the last time.

Rotary Mowers Or Reel Mowers?

Rotary mowers are the typical go-to option, as they are relatively inexpensive, quickly mow your lawn, and only require some basic maintenance. However, rotary mowers are unable to cut grass lower than 1 inch, assuming that you wanted to cut your grass that low. Additionally, rotary mowers don't leave as clean of a cut as reel mowers.

Rotary mowers come in a range of options including gas-powered, electric, and battery-operated. Gas-powered rotary mowers offer the greatest power, but electric and battery-operated rotary mowers are lighter and quieter.

Reel mowers cut the grass with a different technique, more like scissors, rather than a spinning blade. This allows them to cut cleanly so you can cut your lawn at the lowest possible setting. Reel mowers come in manual or power options. Typically, reel mowers are only used when cutting grass at heights of 2 inches or below.

Edging And Trimming Your Lawn

After you get done mowing, now is a good time to edge your lawn to give your perimeter a nice clean look. Either a manual or power edger does the job just fine. Typically, you won't need to edge your lawn every time you mow, just do so when the grass starts to grow out in places where it shouldn't, like over your driveway.

In places where it is hard to reach with the mower, use a trimmer to cut your lawn a uniform length throughout. Working with a power trimmer takes some practice in order to cut at a uniform height. If you don't have a power trimmer, you can use manual shears that will get the job done, albeit slowly.

Cleaning Up After Cutting Your Lawn

After cutting your lawn, trimming, and edging, it is time to clean up all of the debris. Start by removing lawn clippings from driveways and pathways with a broom or a power blower. Ideally, place these lawn clippings back on your lawn to maintain nitrogen levels.

Turning Your Lawn Into Art

Ever since I attended my first Major League Baseball game, I was fascinated by the stripes in the outfield and wondered why no one else's grass looked like that in my neighborhood. This is how I first was introduced to striping and the potential for turning an ordinary lawn into an art masterpiece.

109

Striping Your Lawn

Striping is simply bending all the grass blades in a specific direction so the light bounces off them making them look uniform. Striping your grass is as simple as rolling your grass after you mow or adding a roller or a striper onto your lawnmower. After your lawnmower cuts your grass, a roller that follows the lawnmower pushes all the grass blades in a certain direction. As you make your way back up your lawn on the next row, the roller pushes the grass blades in the opposite direction. This causes the stripe appearance, as row after row of grass is bent in contrary directions.

If you don't have access to a roller or don't have the roller attachment for your lawnmower, you can also use a drag mat or lawn sweeper to make these stripes. However, if you are serious about striping your lawn every time you mow, the lawnmower attachment is the way to go.

Striping your lawn all comes down to personal preference, as you can add in any pattern you want, but the most common is the diamond pattern and the plaid pattern. Whatever design pattern you choose, start with the boundary of your property, assuming it is in a straight line, and continue using this reference so your stripes are as straight as can be. If you are running the lawnmower over a spot that was already cut, either lift up the front end or disengage the blades so it isn't being mowed twice.

If you really want to expand your horizons, you can draw and write images or words into your lawn depending on how you stripe it. Obviously, this will take some practice to get right but if you are committed to your craft, your lawn can say everything you want about you. For more complex lawn art, you will need a hand roller that you use after you mow your grass.

CHAPTER 7 -
WEEDS, PESTS, AND DISEASE
CONTROL

The battle between weeds, pests, and diseases is always going to be a grueling war that has no end. However, if you remain vigilant, you will be able to keep these invaders at bay before they take over your yard.

DEALING WITH WEEDS

Weeds come in all different varieties, some are annuals, meaning they grow from seed every single year, while others are biennials and perennials, meaning they live 2 years or more than 3 years respectively.

Perennial weeds are the hardest weeds to remove, as they simply go dormant just like grass, and come back when the weather is better. If these weeds aren't removed from your lawn they will continuously grow and for all intents and purposes, never die.

Not only do perennials spread by seed, but they also spread by expanding their rhizomes, meaning that the entire plant needs to be killed off in order to eliminate them.

Examples of perennial weeds include quackgrass, dandelion, and white clover.

Annual weeds, the most infamous being crabgrass and annular bluegrass, are a bit easier to deal with if they are stopped before they have a chance to germinate.

Defend Your Lawn From Weeds By Mowing Regularly

You heard it before and yes, it is true, mowing your lawn is the most important aspect of weed inhibition. If you are already mowing your lawn every time it gets slightly above the cut height, you probably won't have many weeds to deal with.

On the other hand, if you cut your lawn too low in hopes of reducing the number of times you have to cut your grass over the year, weeds are bound to grow quickly, as the grass is too low to shade out developing weeds. Avoid mowing your lawn low and stick to a regular schedule of mowing that ensures your grass is consistently high enough to block out weeds.

Properly Fertilizing Your Lawn Protects Against Weeds

Fertilizing your lawn in spring and late fall is one way to push out weeds like crabgrass in cool-climate lawns. On the other hand, warm-climate grasses should be fertilized in the summer when they are growing the fastest, yet not in the early spring or fall when weeds are more likely to use that fertilizer for energy.

Watering Your Lawn Properly
Reduces Weeds

As stated before, water your lawn thoroughly yet infrequently. Typically, weed seeds won't germinate when the soil is thoroughly watered infrequently, as they sit on the surface and would prefer a constant source of water. The less frequently you water your lawn gives you the upper hand when it comes to the battle against weeds.

Herbicides

Aside from the natural preventatives listed above, if weeds get out of control, it's time to turn to chemical assistance.

Pre-emergent Herbicides

The idea behind pre-emergent herbicides is that weed seeds are not allowed to germinate so they can never become established plants. Pre-emergent herbicides are extremely effective when applied in the spring, allowing the grass to grow quickly without competing against germinating weed seeds. Apply pre-emergent herbicides when soil temperatures are between 50°F and 55°F to give your lawn a head start on weeds.

Post-emergent Herbicides

After weeds have already developed, post-emergent herbicides are the go-to option. However, at this point, once weeds have already become established, they are harder to remove. Ideally, select a post-emergent selective herbicide that is specific to the weed you are targeting and spray it directly on the weed, instead of covering your entire lawn.

If however, you are dealing with many different types of weeds, it may be better to use a non-selective herbicide that will simply kill all vegetative material. This non-selective herbicide can't be applied to the entire lawn, as it would kill off everything. Only use this if your goal is to eliminate all vegetation before renovating your lawn.

The Difference Between Contact And Systemic Herbicides

Contact herbicides only kill the part of the plant it is applied to. For instance, spraying contact herbicide on the leaves will kill off the leaves, but not the root system.

On the other hand, systemic herbicides are absorbed directly into the plant and kill the entire plant all the way down to the root system.

Safety Precautions When Using Herbicides And Other Chemicals

Before using chemical herbicides, read the warnings on the bottle and get familiar with the chemical you are about to use. When applying chemical herbicides, wear protective equipment, apply it when the wind is at a minimum, and clean off the equipment and safety equipment, as well as your boots after use.

114

I Don't Want To Use Chemicals, What Are The Organic Options For Killing Weeds?

While organic options for killing weeds aren't quite as good as the chemical equivalents, they do exist. First, pulling weeds out by hand is a time-tested solution for removing weeds, at least temporarily. Unfortunately, if you have a lot of weeds to pull out, this isn't a lower back-friendly solution.

Corn Gluten Meal Herbicide

As far as a pre-emergent herbicide, corn gluten meal is the best organic option. Simply placing the corn gluten meal onto your lawn roughly 1 month to 1 1/2 months before weed seeds begin to germinate can stop them from germination. Using corn gluten meal as a pre-emergent herbicide is a multi-year approach, but if you do it every year within 4 years you shouldn't have any more dandelions.

As far as post-emergent organic herbicides, using vinegar or boiling water can kill weeds that are already established. Simply pour vinegar or boiling water onto weeds and watch them wither away. Both of these techniques are non-selective, so they will kill your grass near the weeds.

DEALING WITH PESTS

Lawns that are properly maintained generally don't have serious pest issues. This is why it is so important to properly water, mow, and fertilize your lawn as we discussed earlier. Additionally, dethatching and core aerating your lawn on a regular basis is the key to keeping insects at bay, as they often live in the thatch area, as it offers them protection.

The ability to deal with pests promptly separates amazing lawns from mediocre lawns. Both insects and mammals want an easy snack. Some insects eat the grass, others suck the juice out of the grass, while others eat the root system. Mammals like raccoons and moles don't eat the grass, but they burrow into the lawn looking for food. In any case, be prepared to deal with pests as they arise.

The key to dealing with pests is to be vigilant and quickly address the issue as soon as you notice it. Ideally, look over your grass on a daily basis, searching for signs of damage. A visual inspection from afar is not enough, you will have to get down on the ground level, ideally with a magnifying glass, to see exactly what is going on. As soon as you see some insects munching on your lawn realize that more are soon to join them.

Natural Insect Control

The best way to reduce the population of harmful insects is to use biological control, meaning that other insects that feed on harmful insects are added to the lawn. In this way, you won't have to use any noxious chemicals that may cause more damage than good.

Nematodes As Pest Control

There are certain nematodes that love to feast on a wide range of lawn pests. These nematodes eat grubs, sod webworms, and cutworms.

Bacillus thuringiensis (BT) Pest Control

There are also bacterial aids that can kill off these worms, known as *Bacillus thuringiensis* (BT). Generally, a mixture of BT and water is sprayed in multiple applications over a couple of weeks to kill off pathogenic worm populations.

Endophytic Fungi Pest Control

There are also certain fungi that can be introduced into a new lawn that naturally repel insects. Typically, these endophytic fungi are added to grass seeds so both your grass and fungi grow together symbiotically.

Pyrethrin Pest Control

There are certain natural pesticides like pyrethrin, made from the Chrysanthemum plant. This pesticide is not only natural but extremely strong and should only be used on spots that are damaged by pests, not sprayed on the entire lawn.

Neem Pest Control

Neem is another plant extract that can kill Japanese beetles.

Insecticidal Soap Pest Control

There are certain soaps known as insecticidal soaps that can kill grubs, chinch bugs, billbugs, and the infamous sod webworm. Typically, mix insecticidal soap with water and spray it over your entire lawn, leaving you with a non-toxic and biodegradable insecticide.

Chemical Insecticides

There is a wide range of chemical insecticides on the market and they generally offer the most efficient method for killing off pests for the lowest cost. Realize that many of these chemical pesticides are toxic to people and other mammals so it is important to stay off your lawn and keep your dog off your lawn after applying these chemicals.

Gamma-Cyhalothrin

Gamma-Cyhalothrin, sold under the brand name, Spectracide Triazicide Insect Killer, is a chemical pesticide that kills nearly all lawn insect pests. One application can control pests for 3 months.

Trichlorfon

Trichlorfon, sold under the brand name Dylox, is a chemical pesticide that kills cutworms, sod webworms, billbugs, white grubs, and chinch bugs.

Carbaryl

Carbaryl, sold under the brand name Sevin, is a chemical pesticide that is used to kill white grubs and billbugs.

Fipronil

Fipronil, sold under the brand name Taurus SC, is a chemical pesticide that is used to kill ants.

DEALING WITH INSECTS

The goal isn't to kill all insects, as they aren't all considered pests, and attempting to do so is an impossibility. However, as soon as the damage threshold of a pest is breached, your lawn will suffer.

Identifying Insect Pests

The key is to identify the insects that are causing damage to your lawn so you can take targeted action against them. The typical insect pests you are going to come across include white grubs, the sod webworm, army worms, chinch bugs, billbugs, cutworms, greenbugs, mole cricket, and ants.

White Grubs

When white grubs start feasting on your lawn, brown patches of grass that are irregularly shaped will form. Typically, this infestation happens in the late spring and early fall seasons. The turf that is damaged will be easy to separate from the soil. When white grubs are present, mammals, like raccoons will be more inclined to burrow into your lawn in search of a meal.

Treatment against white grubs includes using nematodes, Gamma-Cyhalothrin, Trichlorfon, or carbaryl.

Sod Webworms

Sod webworms will also cause dry, irregularly shaped patches on your lawn. Typically, sod webworms attack the driest parts of your lawn first. These worms eat the grass at night and tunnel into the thatch during the daytime.

The best way to treat sod webworms is to use BT, pyrethrin, Gamma-Cyhalothrin, Trichlorfon, or carbaryl.

Army Worms

Army worms eat the grass during the nighttime and burrow into the thatch during the daytime.

The typical treatment for army worms is BT, Gamma-Cyhalothrin, Trichlorfon, or planting grass seeds that contain endophyte fungi.

Chinch Bugs

Chinch bugs don't eat the grass, but rather, they suck the juice out of it, killing it off. Chinch bugs are identified by brown grass patches that are circular, not irregularly shaped. Typically, chinch bugs start their feast in the sunniest, hottest areas of your lawn.

Treating chinch bugs is typically done with insecticidal soaps or Gamma-Cyhalothrin. Additionally, planting grass that contains endophyte fungi is a great prophylactic measure against chinch bugs.

Billbugs

Billbug larvae feast on the grass, resulting in circular brown patches.

Treating a billbug infestation is accomplished by using neem, carbaryl, or Gamma-Cyhalothrin.

Cutworms

Cutworms eat the grass near the root level. A large number of cutworms need to be present to severely damage the lawn.

To treat a cutworm infestation, use BT, Gamma-Cyhalothrin, Trichlorfon, pyrethrin, or carbaryl.

Greenbugs

Greenbugs are often identified by dead grass that looks a bit rusty. Greenbugs suck the juices out of grass blades. Additionally, greenbugs inject toxins into the grass that can end up killing it.

Insecticidal soaps are the best treatment option for greenbugs.

Mole Crickets

Mole Crickets tunnel into the soil and feed on the roots of your grass.

Treatment for mole crickets is best during the springtime. Using nematodes, neem, Gamma-Cyhalothrin, Trichlorfon, or pyrethrin treats the problem.

Ants

Ants, especially fire ants are easily identifiable, as they create mounds of dirt on your lawn. When doing so, they destroy the grass.

Treatment options for fire ants include insecticidal soap and fipronil.

DEALING WITH MAMMALS

Mammals like skunks, raccoons, moles, and armadillos can destroy your lawn by burrowing in it for food. Typically, these animals are only active at night time and are present in packs, resulting in serious damage in a short amount of time.

The key to removing skunks, raccoons, moles, and armadillos from your lawn is to kill the pests, typically white grubs, they are feeding on. After killing off white grubs, these opportunistic eaters will likely look for somewhere else to get a meal.

DEALING WITH DISEASE

Diseases are another issue that can turn your lawn into a horror show. However, anyone who takes care of their lawn by performing consistent maintenance significantly reduces the probability of developing diseases.

Diseases typically take the form of fungi and require three different factors to develop. First, the pathogen must be present, second, the grass must be vulnerable to disease, and third, the right conditions must persist for that fungus to develop.

A healthy lawn has a symbiosis between the soil, micro-organisms, and grass plants. However, when an imbalance is present, conditions for disease to flourish makes it all the more likely.

To maintain that symbiotic balance, mowing, fertilizing, and watering your lawn correctly not only make your grass look excellent, but also provides a barrier against disease.

Properly Mowing Your Lawn

First, make sure the blades on your lawnmower are sharp and only cut off 1/3 of the length at any particular time. This ensures the least amount of stress on your grass, making it more disease resistant.

Properly Fertilizing Your Lawn

Properly fertilizing your lawn at the right time with the appropriate quantities improves plant health, making it more resistant to disease. However, overfertilization is stressful to your lawn, as grass shoots up quickly, while the roots are unable to maintain the same pace. When overfertilizing grass, thatch develops, making it more conducive to disease.

Properly Watering Your Lawn

Watering your lawn thoroughly, yet infrequently gives the grassroots all the water they need for an extended period of time without maintaining constantly wet conditions that are conducive to fungal growth. When watering your lawn, always do so in the morning or afternoon, so it doesn't remain wet overnight, giving fungi optimal conditions.

Avoid Overapplying Pesticides

Over-application of pesticides can allow diseases to develop. Pesticides not only kill off the intended pests, but they are also harmful to microorganisms and other insects that are beneficial to your grass. Applying insecticides stresses your lawn, giving diseases a chance to take a foothold. Ideally, choose a pesticide that is specific to the pest you are looking to kill off to avoid unintended broad microorganism die-off.

Choosing Disease-Resistant Grass Varieties

When starting your lawn from scratch, choose the correct grass species that is perfect for your climate, as a grass species that isn't designed to grow in your area will be susceptible to disease. If you have to, perform an entire lawn renovation to replace your lawn with a hearty grass species.

Remove Thatch Buildup Regularly

Thatch buildup is directly correlated with pests and diseases. When thatch is not removed regularly, it forms a barrier that doesn't allow nutrients and water to reach the soil. Thatch also provides protection from pests and results in damp conditions that are perfect for developing diseases. Additionally, core aerating your lawn on a regular basis reduces damp conditions on the soil surface where fungi are bound to develop.

Identifying Lawn Diseases

If there is something wrong with your lawn, it is imperative to identify the issue. Many people mistakenly jump to the conclusion that a disease is causing a problem with their grass, but it is often drought or pests. To properly identify whether diseases are resulting in the demise of your lawn, analyze closely, again at ground level with a magnifying glass, to get a good look at the issue.

Since identifying diseases is harder than identifying pests, it is often best to contact a professional who deals with lawn diseases on a regular basis. Many times, lawn disease experts will have you send a sample of your lawn to them and return the results of the disease analysis within days. Ideally, give them as much information as possible even if you don't think it is pertinent to the problem at hand. This will allow disease experts to take into account all possible factors when making their assessment.

Fungi Issues

If the results of the disease test come back and indeed your lawn is suffering from a pathogenic fungus, don't jump to conclusions and immediately apply a fungicide. While applying fungicide may be the right choice, these chemicals are extremely stressful on your lawn and there may be better ways to deal with fungi issues. Oftentimes, dealing with fungi issues takes time, as the factors that resulted in fungal growth need to be addressed so the problem doesn't return. If the problem is extreme and the only solution is to apply a fungicide, apply one specific to the fungal species you are dealing with.

Common Types Of Diseases

There are a number of common diseases including Brown Patch, Leaf Spot, Dollar Spot, Pythium Blight, Fusarium Blight, Snow Mold, Powdery Mildew, Red Thread, Rust, and Stripe Smut.

DEALING WITH DEAD SPOTS

Dead spots can come from pests, dogs, chemical spills like gasoline or fertilizer, or diseases. The process of repairing dead spots is similar no matter what the cause.

Repairing Dog Spots

While most people don't consider their family dog to be a pest, dogs certainly damage the grass. Aside from getting rid of your dog completely, there are no easy solutions to dealing with the damage they cause. As such, be ready to fix the dead spots they leave behind.

If you are extremely observant, go out after your dog has urinated on the grass and water down these spots heavily to dilute them. Unfortunately, you are not going to get every place they have urinated so dead spots on your lawn are inevitable. Dealing with dog spots promptly is essential to avoid an infestation of weeds and improve your curb appeal.

Seeding A Dead Spot

Start by digging out all the dead grass in a circle or square pattern. Now, remove the topsoil in that area and replace it with non-contaminated topsoil. When doing so, level it out and ensure that it is at the same level as the soil throughout the rest of your lawn if you intend to grow the grass from seeds.

When seeding a previous dead spot, follow the seeding rate as indicated by the label on the side of the bag of grass seeds. Typically, a hand spreader is perfect to apply seeds for this small-scale application. Then, apply a starter fertilizer, rake in, and compact the seeds down so they have the greatest contact with the soil. After that, add straw over the area to protect the seeds and water it like you would with a newly seeded lawn.

Replacing A Dead Spot With Sod

If you intend to use a piece of sod to fill in the dead spot, calculate the soil level, depending on how thick the sod is so it lines up flush when you insert the sod. Typically, the soil level will be around 1 inch lower than the rest of your lawn.

After sacrificing a piece of sod from another area of your lawn, place it into the hole and line it up like a puzzle piece. If you cut it out exactly it should look completely flush with the rest of your lawn. Now, water it well so the roots grow in quickly.

CHAPTER 8 - EXPERT LAWN TIPS FOR COMMON LAWN CARE PROBLEMS

Let's go over a number of common lawn care problems and solutions to these issues.

My Grass Doesn't Grow In Shady Areas - Planting And Caring For Your Lawn In Shady Areas

If your entire lawn receives direct sunlight, you won't have to worry about dealing with shady areas and getting grass to fill into these areas. However, if you are like most people, you want a few trees on your property and some other shady areas that fill out the landscaping.

If certain areas of your lawn don't receive at least 6 hours of direct sunlight a day, it is best to plant a different species of grass in these areas. In locations that have cold climate grasses, something like Fine Fescue is appropriate. In locations where hot climate grasses are growing, Saint Augustine grass is known to be relatively shade tolerant. While planting a different species of grass will clearly stand out from the rest of your lawn, if you want to fill in these shady areas with grass, you will have to accept this reality.

Grass in shady areas won't require as much irrigation or fertilizer as the rest of your lawn. As a general rule, apply 10% less fertilizer to grass in shady areas than you apply on the rest of your lawn. This will ensure that it doesn't grow too fast and become susceptible to disease. Additionally, reduce foot traffic in shady areas as much as possible.

Allow grass grown in shady areas to grow a bit higher than the rest of your lawn before cutting it. For instance, if you cut your lawn at 2 1/2 inches, raise your lawnmower's cut height to 3 inches for grass located in shady areas.

Adding a biostimulant to grass planted in shady areas increases the number of amino acids, hormones, and vitamins available to it so it doesn't have to produce these factors on its own, allowing shady grass to conserve energy.

Another tool of the trade is to use a growth regulator like Primo, as it limits the amount of vertical growth. A growth regulator allows grass to utilize its energy to improve its root system and rhizomes instead of growing foliage. This causes grass treated with a growth regulator to grow horizontally more than it grows vertically.

Having Trees And A Beautiful Lawn - The Best Of Both Worlds

Having an amazing lawn with no trees whatsoever doesn't make for much curb appeal. However, trees create shady areas that will stunt grass growth and even kill off many varieties of grass. How can I have a beautiful yard with trees in it?

Some people plant trees and place stones, gravel, or some other type of cover over their soil instead of grass so they don't have to worry about the health of their lawns in these areas. While that is fine, there are ways to grow trees and a decent lawn underneath them.

As soon as a tree is getting to the point where it is blocking out the sunlight, it is important to prune it so light can pass through and reach the grass below.

If there isn't much light reaching the grass, you will have to plant a type of grass seed that is perfect for shady areas, something like Fine Fescue in cold climates and Saint Augustine grass in warm climates.

Before planting just any type of tree, check with the local nursery and ask them which types of trees grow best in your area.

Realize that your lawn and trees are competing for nutrients, sunlight, and water. It is important to overwater in areas that contain trees so the lawn doesn't dry out. While your lawn should be watered thoroughly yet infrequently, realize that trees need far more water because their root system is far deeper than your lawn. In general, you should focus on watering your lawn to a depth of about 7 inches, but in areas with trees, water must soak into the soil around 3 ft deep so the roots have access to it.

Ideally, create a buffer zone between trees and your lawn. Typically, place a circle barrier around a tree dependent on its size, and fill that area in with wood chips, rocks, or plants that don't require lots of sunlight. This will make it easier to care for your lawn and your tree, as you won't have to mow near your tree and it will make the overall process of mowing easier.

When watering your lawn and your trees, adjust your sprinklers so the water sprays near the base of the tree, but not actually hitting the trunk directly. If the water continuously has contact with the trunk of the tree, it can result in fungal diseases.

Fixing Uneven Spots Throughout Your Lawn

If you have unsightly and annoying uneven spots in your lawn, there is a way to level out these areas without having to completely renovate your lawn. Obviously, you will have to renovate that small area so do so when it is the perfect time to plant sod depending on your climate, as we've discussed earlier.

First, remove the grass in the uneven area with a spade as you would if you were running a sod farm. Ideally, cut it in a square formation, and remove the sod leaving at least one inch of soil attached to it. Wet the sod you just removed and roll it up to prevent dehydration.

Now, level out the soil, keeping in mind the 1 inch of soil on the sod. Now, water the bare soil and place the sod back in it, fitting it in like a puzzle piece. If it doesn't line up exactly, remove or add soil and find a position where it is completely level. Now, water the sod on a regular basis, ideally once a day until it roots into the soil and looks like the rest of your lawn.

How Do I Deal With Soil Composition Issues?

Dealing with soil composition issues can be a tricky undertaking, especially if you don't get a soil test to tell you exactly what your soil contains. However, it may be obvious that your soil isn't going to provide a solid foundation for your grass. For example, if your soil is excessively clay dominant, it may be best to just buy topsoil in dump truck loads and fill in your lawn with this nutrient-rich medium.

On the other hand, if only certain small amendments need to be made to your soil to bring it into ideal composition, get a soil test and make the adjustments scientifically based on the analysis.

What Do I Do When There's A Drought?

If you are enduring drought-like conditions and want to maintain your lawn's green luster, you will be forced to water your grass to maintain the minimum 1 inch of water per week guideline. Ideally, try to get the entire 1 inch of water on your lawn in one or two applications so the water seeps deeper into the soil where it won't immediately evaporate.

If there is a mandate against using water on your lawn in your area, you may be able to use the gray water that comes out of your house. Using this gray water to irrigate your lawn may be the difference between a lawn that remains green and one that dies off completely.

Fertilize your lawn less during a drought, as your grass won't be able to use that fertilizer if there isn't an adequate amount of water available. Specifically, reduce the amount of nitrogen you apply to your lawn during a drought.

Additionally, mow your lawn at a higher height to reduce stress on your grass and protect the soil by maintaining more moisture.

If your lawn starts to turn brown, you have a choice to make, either fight against Mother Nature by irrigating, applying the micronutrient iron that helps maintain the green color or just throw in the towel and allow your lawn to go dormant.

If you take the latter route and just allow your lawn to go dormant for a couple of weeks don't fret, it will return to full vigor once the rain returns. If you are going through a severe drought where your grass dies off completely, you will have a good excuse to start from scratch and renovate it with an ideal grass species when the moment is right.

There are even some paints out there that can be applied to brown grass to make it look green. I personally wouldn't recommend that because to me that is like putting lipstick on a pig.

What Should I Do About The Leaves That Fall In My Yard?

It is important to remove the leaves that fall on your yard, as they block out sunlight and reduce airflow to your grass. Ideally, either rake leaves up or collect them in the bag attachment on your lawnmower.

Then, place those leaves on a compost pile along with your other grass clippings. If you have a garden, leaves are the perfect source of organic matter that can provide free nutrition to your vegetables.

CONCLUSION

There you have it, no matter what you want to do with your lawn, whether it's seeding it from scratch, renovating it, or just maintaining it, you have the information you need to do it correctly.

Remember, lawn perfection isn't only about selecting an ideal type of grass seed for your lawn, it's about optimizing your soil, properly watering your lawn, fertilizing your lawn adequately, and mowing your lawn on a regular basis, not only for the season but for years to come.

If you stick to the maintenance guidelines presented in this book, from dethatching, core aeration, overseeding, applying both pre-emergent and post-emergent herbicides when necessary, and ensuring that your lawn has everything it needs to grow optimally, it will no doubt look its best.

More important than anything else, enjoy the journey, take a moment to inhale a deep breath after caring for your lawn, and hold it in for a second or two. While the final results are inevitably going to be directly related to the amount of work you put into your lawn, enjoying the moment is ultimately what lawn care and more importantly, life, is all about.

Thank you for reading *Lawn Perfection! A Golf Course Superintendent's Guide To Home Lawn Care And Maintenance*. If you enjoyed it, please rate it on Amazon and tell others you think would benefit from the information contained in this book.

Until next time, may Mother Nature smile upon you, and may your lawnmower keep rolling until infinity.

REFERENCES

▶ Mellor, D. R. (2003). *The Lawn Bible: How to Keep It Green, Groomed, and Growing Every Season of the Year* (1st ed.). Hachette Books.

▶ Walheim, L. (1998). *Lawn Care for Dummies* (1st ed.). For Dummies.

▶ *Lawn Guides*. (n.d.). YouTube. https://www.youtube.com/playlist?list=PLzripA58GQvEzNUfQjb5t_Cg18HvLboo7

▶ *How To Soil Test*. (n.d.). YouTube. https://www.youtube.com/playlist?list=PLzripA58GQvFAHwnvBrR9OweEin9WV-4j

▶ *Lawn Leveling*. (n.d.). YouTube. https://www.youtube.com/playlist?list=PLzripA58GQvHyzv3A-LoKbhBdNUqxOvt1

▶ *Irrigation and Sprinklers*. (n.d.). YouTube. https://www.youtube.com/playlist?list=PLzripA58GQvGGeg_TAh6WA4V2z8hIrd3O

▶ *Spring Lawn Care*. (n.d.). YouTube. https://www.youtube.com/playlist?list=PLzripA58GQvEYXxEvC8xROGnIjiL1DjIW

▶ *Summer Lawn Care*. (n.d.). YouTube. https://www.youtube.com/playlist?list=PLzripA58GQvE3txM8dAp0xzPnKd6jXrAI

▶ *Fall Lawn Care Program*. (n.d.). YouTube. https://www.youtube.com/playlist?list=PLzripA58GQvFc_O_Oy_LcrVzthjb08QDi

▶ *Lawn Renovation*. (n.d.). YouTube. https://www.youtube.com/playlist?list=PLzripA58GQvHb7OCzWrvmCcan8g4Sz0WR

▶ Ryan Knorr Lawn Care. (2020, April 19). *Easy Ways to REPAIR DOG DAMAGE and BARE SPOTS In The Lawn*. YouTube. https://www.youtube.com/watch?v=S4oJzu1Hfkc

▶ *Lawn Care 101: Your Seasonal Guide to Lawn Care & Maintenance*. (n.d.). https://www.wikilawn.com/lawn-care/

- *What is Post Emergent Herbicide | Complete Guide.* (2022, January 27). Farmingeo. https://farmingeo.com/post-emergent-herbicide/

- *When is the Best Time to Lay Sod?* (2022, June 17). Sod Solutions. https://sod-solutions.com/lawn-care-guides/when-is-the-best-time-to-lay-sod/

- Reeves, W. (2020, June 21). *Pre-emergent – When To Apply | Walter Reeves: The Georgia Gardener.* Walter Reeves: The Georgia Gardener | Gardening Tips and Advice From the Most Respected Garden Guru in the Southeast. https://www.walterreeves.com/tools-and-chemicals/pre-emergent-when-to-apply/

- *Topdressing a Lawn: The Benefits and How to Do It.* (2022, July 7). Lawnstarter. https://www.lawnstarter.com/blog/lawn-care-2/guide-topdressing-lawn-grass/

- Runkle, L. (2019, September 3). *What Is Dethatching? The Secret Trick for a Beautiful Lawn.* Real Estate News & Insights | realtor.com®. https://www.realtor.com/advice/home-improvement/what-is-dethatching-your-lawn/

Printed in Great Britain
by Amazon